positive energy

'YINKA AKINTUNDE

positive energy

'YINKA AKINTUNDE

RESOURCE HOUSE LTD.
LONDON

POSITIVE ENERGY

ISBN: 978-1-9161661-0-3

*First Published 2019 by
RESOURCE HOUSE LTD.*

*rh@drakintunde.com
www.drakintunde.com*

· CONTENTS

Disclaimer

This book is a self-help guide based on what the author holds as facts and values. The interpretation and application of the content is absolutely of the reader's volition and choice.

The author or the publisher shall not in any way be liable for the interpretation, application, and outcome of taking the facts and values espoused in this book on board by anyone.

Resource House.
Publisher of POSITIVE ENERGY.

The concept of positive energy is not about perfection. It is not about not having negative thoughts or even being caught up with occasional negativity. It is about not allowing negativity to become your default. You will encounter many failures on your journey of self-imposed self-improvement, but working on self is worth the pain. You will come out refined and of more value on the other side of the furnace.

One main challenge you will deal with in your lifetime is negativity. You will come across it within yourself, your family, in friendships, at school, in your larger community, the city or nation, and work place. You will see the bitterness of negativity in journalism, politics, religion, and even in sports and popular culture. You will see good intentions ruined by negativity and wonder what has gone wrong with our world.

There is so much toxicity all over the place that you will almost be tempted to interpret negativity as a virtue until you truly analyse the undesirable consequences it breeds where it festers.

You are by now, I am sure, tired of all the negativity and its effects, not just on individual morale but on your community and the world at large. Bad energy spreads so quickly and ferociously. It is so common in our world that we could almost be erroneously convinced that negativity and negative people actually outnumber positivity and the positive people.

This can be an adventure in detoxification and maximum imbibition of positivity for you. It is not a do-it-all holy grail of happiness and success, but it is aimed at helping the humanity in you to better evolve, make you a happier person in life, help you to channel and utilise your energy more productively.

Are you looking at the possibility of improving the happenings around you? This book will challenge you to look inward to make the very hard decisions of filtering what you allow into your aura as energy with its accompanying influence.

Negativity is just one of the many manifestations of the negative energy the atmosphere reeks most with these days. It is so much easier to hate and destroy in our world today than ever before, despite the global village we ought to be cohabiting in. The good news is that you don't have to put up with the negativity for one more day. You can take over your aura and fence it with the reinforced wall of positive energy twenty-four/seven.

Energy can be recognised, differentiated, and channelled the right way for the desired result, goal, and effect. You can propagate positive energy and make it common wherever you are. It is high time you take over your aura and the nearby aura being used for negativity around you until our lives, families, communities, and the world at large become a better place of dwelling for mankind.

It is my desire for you to be happy, successful, and find the right drive for living, which by responsibility makes it my assignment to lay the facts before you and help you take responsibility as well.

Have you ever wondered why you think and act the way you do, why you get the kind of result you have, and why you are always treated the way you get treated? These are precipitations of the kind of energy you aggregate, dissipate, and ultimately are left with to dispense in your dealings. You ultimately build a lifestyle around your energy and get results from it.

When you feel helpless about life, you need to know what you can control and what is outside your control. The reality is that what you are in control of in your life is far more important and is of greater impact than what lies outside of your control. One is your energy profile, both in charge and quantum.

- You will be shown how to take charge of your own aura.
- How to generate the right kind of vibes.
- How to channel the available energy for your desired result.
- Learn how to turn the curve.
- Make the right and proper energy migration.
- Get equipped for total switch over.
- See 32 vital energy lessons for living.
- Question yourself on more than 150 markers of positive and negative energy.
- Use energy indices to assess and improve.

The book is small in size enough for you to have an intimate attachment to it; it's also big enough in content for you to load up for your next great move from it.
I wish you a happy reading.

Dr. Yinka Akintunde
May 2019.

·INTRODUCTION

Energy, simply put, is the enablement to get work done. Every form of life on earth utilizes energy for existence. Energy is in a continuous cycle of use for thriving, progress, and productivity. In material form, energy is mostly intangible and invisible, but the impact of energy is undeniable, whether bad or good.

All biological life on our planet is centred around the sun, simply because the sun is a hot ball of immense energy from which most quanta on earth emanate.

Time and seasons are determined by the relative position of the earth to the sun, which is the energy source. This underscores the importance of energy exposure and how the way you utilise your energy can determine the times and seasons of your life.

The engagement of energy will knowingly or unknowingly produce an effect, but the nature and the desirability of such effect depends on the kind of energy engaged. Some effects may be anticipated while others are not. The non-anticipation of effects will not stop it from happening once the needed energy is activated to trigger the effect. Life is full of many unpleasant surprises, and they are most times the actual reflections of the type and level of energy we engage with.

The automation in result generation is frightening and puts innocence in a pale, inconsequential background when life's outcome is being determined. When an electric button is pressed, you don't need to know what it's meant to do nor how it ought to do it before the effect is realised. A process wired into the circuit has been triggered once the button is pressed. The components of the circuit have been activated for an errand, and the effect will thereafter manifest.

As you engage energy in your daily living, automation of effects already wired into the circuit of life are generated. Either you desire such effects or not. These impacts and effects are the stark realities of our lives.

Being happy or sad, progressive or otherwise are to a large extent determined by the shade of energy we bring into daily living.

There is a concept of labelling the energy you engage in daily living as either positive or negative. We will do such in this book and help you generate better and greater desirable effects in your life.

THE CONCEPT OF POSITIVE ENERGY

Chapter One

THE CONCEPT OF POSITIVE ENERGY

Same Quantum but Different Charges

The thin line of demarcation between *justice* and *revenge* makes both sometimes look, feel, and even sound alike, but they are different. Whereas justice seeks to rectify and forestall the wrong, revenge seeks to get even with the wrong, even if it has to be wrongly achieved. The driving energies behind justice and revenge may be the same in intensity or quantum, but they are different in charges they carry and hence the impacts they generate.

Justice is driven by positive energy, but revenge is driven by negative energy. The impacts are different for both the one seeking either and the one against which either is being sought.
How much energy you apply at getting things done is important, but much more important is the charge the energy carries, whether negative charge or positive charge. The effects will tell us the story.

The first law of energy is that it cannot be created but converted. You likely do not need more energy to get things done and produce the desired effects in your life, but you likely need to change the charge of the ones you currently have.

Lesson #1
- A shift in charge rather than a change in quantity may help you get the right result.

Visible Effects

Energy is the ability to generate effects. In the science of nature, we have the primary energy, which is referred to as the potential or inherent energy that lies within an object, such as we have in cells waiting to be channelled. Such can be used to generate motion, electricity, sound, or even nuclear effects.
Even though energy is invisible and mostly inherent, the effects are almost always visible. Such visible effects are the tell-tale signs of what form of energy was utilised. We can even guess how much of such energy was engaged and for how long was it engaged.

Energy Profile

Your personality carries a certain kind of energy signature. It is profiled into your name, presence, image, and creations. This energy profile carries your aura wherever it shows up. It elicits certain kinds of reactions once it is brought out.

The energy profile of stars is what the advertising world thrives on. Advertisers pay billions of dollars annually to import the aura of well-received celebrities into their products' aura in order to trigger an explosion of acceptance. Well-accepted celebrities are kept on board of brands for as long as possible because their exit may mean exportation of the imported aura, and, trust me, the crowd follows the aura.

There is no doubt that these well-received celebrities have taken time in a certain vocation to build a signature positive energy profile. Whatever product or service they are associated with is projected in the light of their aura of acceptance. Their winning in games and sport, angelic model looks, pristine line delivery, show business personality, and other forms of outlook that generated the positive energy aura are now projected as being accessible to us through the products they endorse. Brands are quick to drop the fallen ones like a hot potato when the same celebrity energy profile is filled with enough negative energy to trigger an explosion of rejection.

This same energy profile is what leaders trade with in winning confidence, followership, and getting the job done. Accepted leaders import their energy profile into whatever they are involved in to create an aura of positivity and possibility among the people they lead. They are, therefore, given the chance or benefit of the doubt to lead on.

You are subconsciously building an energy profile for yourself, which literally brings your aura wherever you are represented. This is why it is possible for a letter or resume to be sent in your name and exert great influence. When your name or image comes to a place, a certain kind of energy profile is reflected. It simply mirrors the memory of the last energy deposit you made on your last visit. With people and places where you have not yet made an impression, know with certainty that you are leaving an energy footprint in your interactions. This creates your ultimate energy profile. Help yourself erase negative footprints and build positive ones in your energy profile with people and in places. It will help you live a happier and better life.

Potential Energy

Inside every living thing is the vital force of energy through which life is dispensed as aroma like a sprayed perfume. Human energy for living is the life sustaining driving force with which we make each day of our existence count.

Going forward or drifting backward in life is a reflection of the propelling energy and its utilization. Soaring upward or sinking downward all point to the dominant energy at work within our lives. There is positive and negative energy. They are ultimately revealed by the effect they exert and the ultimate outcome derived.

A person carrying sufficient positive energy will thrive within and dominate a negative environment. The results in such people's lives will be at variance with all the negativity around them. Whereas a person full of negative energy will quickly mess up a positive environment and turn a fruitful garden to a desert without an oasis. There is energy within you in potential form waiting to be charged, harvested, and utilized.

Aura of Energy

There is an invisible space around you. It follows your person and dictates your motions in life. Every human aura is loaded with energy, and no energy is ultimately neutral. Positive and negative energy are revealed by their driving effects on the carrier. You will at some point have a good share of both. There is always a build-up of both the positive and negative energy with both seeking to control you. Personal adjustment, learning, and the choices you make will ultimately determine which energy will eventually dominate you and ultimately charge your aura. Without sounding esoteric, your aura of energy determines what ultimately happens around you.

The dominant energy is revealed in the outcome; the good news is that you can always adjust your energy charge based on your desired result.

Lesson # 2
- Your energy profile can open or shut doors in your face.

CULTIVATING POSITIVE ENERGY FOR GOOD RESULTS

Chapter Two

CULTIVATING POSITIVE ENERGY FOR GOOD RESULTS

Sal was the branch leader when the company faced a very serious threat of collapse as a result of nosediving sales, an aftermath of the negative ripples created for them by a fierce competitor in the industry. Staff morale was down by the turn of events and the extremely negative effect on sales. The fear and trepidation of losing their jobs, homes, even the entire livelihoods with the fearful reality that they may soon not be able to afford such necessities as children's school fees and medical insurance, was palpable in the office.

Sal came into the office everyday with his head bowed, his mood dark, and no clue as to how to get the workers to match their competitor in product quality, service delivery, or customer satisfaction. Figures kept going down on negative projections for forty weeks, and shutting down the branch was imminent until Dave showed up as a secondment from the head office.

Dave was somewhat of a greenhorn in the industry but sent from the headquarters by the board to assist Sal in any capacity Sal deemed fit. His energy level was soon spotted by Sal, and he was granted a free hand of operation to tackle the challenge head on.

Sal was not expecting much change. He did what he had to do at least as a respite for the overwhelmed staff to appear that something was being done to redeem the situation. Many of them were sceptical and didn't fall for the tactic, but Dave was there to stay anyway, until the company sank or the tide turned. The tide did turn ultimately, sales went up, the competitor was defeated in the struggle for the market share, jobs were retained, and everyone moved on with life in a pleasant way.

Dave did not bring more experience or greater qualifications to the table in this situation. He brought a magical aura of positive energy, which did not change the reality on ground, as it were, but turned the tables for good against the reality on ground. The competitor did not vanish into thin air, but the competition spurred Sal's branch from an average into a top-performing firm. Positive energy that is sufficiently channelled will neutralise negative energy in an environment, turn the tables against opposing forces, and bring pleasant results against all odds.

Lesson #3
- Create an aura of possibility.

Around Dave was an aura of possibility, which soon rubbed off on his boss, Sal. His withdrawal into himself started to fade, and the line of communication and chain of command with the unit supervisors was soon restored. In no time, the same fire was kindled all around the factory and the administrative block. Impossible became nothing. Easy or difficult to achieve was no more the ultimate consideration in any project. It shall be done became the approach to any task to be accomplished. The belief that they would beat their competitor to the market game became engrained in everyone's mindset.

The fear of losing out started fading away. Customer complaints were no longer handled with anger, despise, fear and scepticism but with assurance and boldness that the company could please and retain these customers for future patronage.

The feeling of staff that customers were unnecessarily hard to please soon faded away. It suddenly dawned on them that their clients weren't asking for too much and that it was possible to please them.

Before this, there was this negative aura of conspiracy theory in this company and that the competitor was responsible for most customer complaints, and so, they deemed customers impossible to please.

When it was impossible to exit the door, innovation and tenacity to do it right came in to stay with them.

Lesson #4
- Create the aura of sound speech and good image.

Words and the images did matter in Dave's aura, and so the concept of sending a clear message to existing and would-be customers about why they should be chosen above their competitor was Dave's primary concern.

They started putting up graphics on the company premise to inspire good feelings in the workers about the company. Workers started to see that they were working for a company on the winning side of the fierce industrial competition and not the one about to be overrun by a competitor. These graphics spilled over to the outside word and stayed on the minds of customers.

* *Richard Branson, in his book Finding my Virginity, talked of how Virgin* Airline entered the seemingly sealed and impossible U.S. aviation market clearly dominated by much bigger and well-entrenched indigenous airline. The environment was made so difficult for Virgin by their competitors and accompanying strict regulations. On page 99, Branson describes how they took to the streets of San Francisco in January 2007 with words and images to the American of what they are about and the good they brought to the aviation industry. Five months later, more than 75,000 letters had been sent by the people on the street to Congress to compel fair treatment for Virgin. By August, Virgin's licence of operation in the United State of America. was ultimately released, and a great dream came to fruition against all odds.

In the same book Branson talked about how they do not take off quietly in any new market they come into. They always make a loud entry with the launch bordering on weird in some cases.

Lesson #5
- Load up your aura with good energy memories.

When a perfume is released by squeezing the bottle nozzle, an immediate strong aroma is released, and much sweet fragrance is left behind long after the bottle is empty. Life does not and will not just spray perfume and sweet fragrance in your aura but also the putrid. You will determine which you want to retain and which you want to carry around. The dominant aroma is not necessarily the only aroma. It is just the one allowed to linger.

Even though Dave in the above story was a greenhorn in the company, he was not a greenhorn to the challenges of life. He

11

was a young man who had encountered refusals and suffered rejection. He was a product of a not-very-noble affair between a community leader and an unknown woman. He was almost not wanted by the man and even the mum. He was not invited to most important family gathering in his father's house as his presence would always bring bad memories and set tongues wagging. Dave therefore learned how to take rejection and refusal with a good attitude. He made his own friends, sorted his own acceptance, and grew his own acquaintances without bitterness towards his father or siblings.

Dave did not go to elite schools as his older siblings, but he went to school in any case. He made the most of what he was exposed to as formal and informal education. He developed wit to make up for privileges he lacked. He learned survival in the jungle of life in spite of the predators and landed a not-so-easy job.

In every instance of an opportunity in the face of daunting challenge, Dave was quick to bring out a survival story from his retinue he had gathered over years of struggle.

Fill your aura with the sweet fragrance of victory, and let it linger as memory. Such fragrance doesn't have to be yours. It can be someone's story of triumph. Borrow and spray it in your aura today. Someone will soon borrow yours tomorrow, too.

The world is full of putrid and not-so-pleasant aroma of troubles and defeats. You cannot let them dominate your aura or else you will be miserable, always angry, and frustrated in life.
Put up stickers, place memorabilia, take pictures, play music, audio and videos, visit places that regenerate good memories in you. Smell fragrance that elicit good feeling and bring good

moments to you. Allow the build-up of the positive energy you so desire to bubble up within you with nostalgia.

Lesson #6
- Strive for mastery.

When all of life's efforts are given to and driven towards fighting your enemies, both real and imagined, a thick dark cloud of negative energy will be persistently built around you with every step. This is one of the major reasons people can be making progress and yet be so unhappy to the point of snapping into depression for particularly no obvious reason.

Your main goal in life must be a real battle with yourself towards mastery.
- A pummelling of yourself towards comprehensive capability to deliver your line excellently.
- A conditioning of yourself for unending self-improvement.
- Thorough investments in yourself for continuous evolvement.
- Becoming a master in delivering your line and mandate per phase.

One major operational shift brought by Dave with his arrival is a shift in where efforts are focused in the company's pursuit of change. It had been about beating the opposition until Dave arrived. The drive had always been to checkmate a rival, outshine an opponent, or stop the competitor from out-succeeding them in the market.

Whereas the market is competitive, the real determinants of the equilibrium are the consumers whose satisfaction is pivotal in the war of sales.

"The singular drive to out-please the consumers at all cost is all that we need to out-run everyone in the pack," said Dave at his inaugural meeting with the management staff. We don't need to hate or chase our competitors, neither do we need to be paranoid about their next moves.

Strategic goods and service delivery plans from that point were re-designed without a thought about their competitors. The focus became how to meet the needs of the consumers rather than how to beat the opposition. In time, the tide turned at a good cost but also for a good course when energy was re-focused.
You can only exercise control and take command of your aura and life to the level with which you have mastered delivering your own line or mandate. Otherwise you will be running a rat race set by others and be unhappy because you are being beaten in the race. Being the best, you can be in delivering your line is your deliverance from the rat race that creates unhappiness.

The joy of flying is not just in beating the gravitational force that serves as the inertia of keeping every object on earth. Those who beat the gravitational force to fly don't do so by just fighting the gravity. Gravity is defied by generating an upward lift which is combined with certain quanta of propelling forces for flight. Much, if not all, of the energy generated in an aircraft on flight is channelled towards lifting it up to the desired height and moving it forward at such height to the desired destination. Otherwise flying would be impossible. So, in the initial stages of evolving aviation, much focus was on how to generate such enormous energy in an aircraft and channel it not only for such lift but also for propulsion.

The world is ultimately kept safe today not only because of the wars that have been fought by people and nations with huge arsenals but much more because of the negotiations that have been brokered and compromises that have been reached by the people and nations of goodwill in the heat of conflict. Otherwise the first and the second world wars, among other major battles, would still rage on today and passed from generation to generation.

Much, and if possible, all, of your energy must be to lift not to fight gravity. Gravity is part of the earthly life that cannot be eradicated just as negative events and negative people are part and parcel of life. You will encounter many in marriages, carriers, vocations, neighbourhoods, and many other spheres of interaction. The deterrent is for you to evolve yourself, build your own mastery to master your aura. Every other person can be a contributor but not the owner and determinant of your aura. Determine to fill it up with what lifts upward and propels forward.

From the book "Finding My Virginity" – Richard Branson

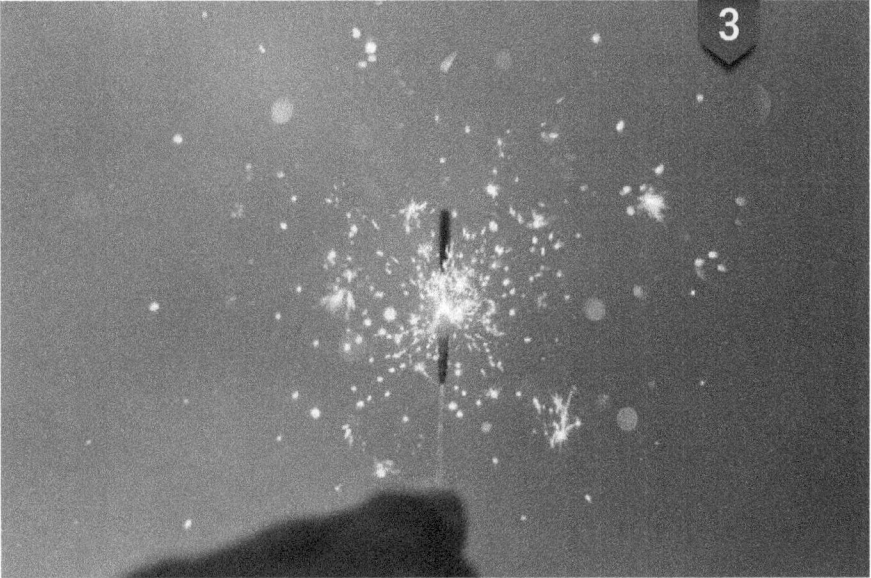

POSITIVE
ENERGY
BY CHOICE

POSITIVE ENERGY BY CHOICE

Lesson #7
- Build up positive energy.

Your assignment is to build up as much positive energy within yourself and make it dominate your aura as much as is it within your power. The choice of what stays within you and dominates your aura as energy is within your control. If there is any power you must not hand over to anyone or anything, it is this choice power. Weigh up its impact on your motion and classify it as negative or positive.

Lesson #8
Defuse negative energy.

In like manner, when you notice the build-up of negativity within you, your assignment is to defuse it and rescue your aura from it as much as you can. The end will always justify the means.

Lesson #9
Not your fault yet

The appearance of negative energy in your aura may not necessarily be your fault. But your allowance and docile accommodation of such to ultimately foul you up is nothing but abdication of your responsibility to look after yourself.

Negative energy and its carrier will make you assume, think, and behave wrongly. They will ultimately make you and bring out the wrong version of you. Your job is to disperse and dismiss them both. Do not tolerate their strong hold on you. Note well that the carrier of negative energy can be a person, place, thing, or event.

Another story has it that Jose was a well-loved young man, the last of a family of five in a far-away community from the east. He was affable, promising, and full of dreams. He was hard working, followed the straight and narrow path with the whole world before him. He made his parent proud, and so much success was expected of him.

Jose's dad took ill after his colourful seventeenth birthday and found no respite for over two decades. Contrary to the young man's drive and desire to study electrical engineering in the university, the longevity of his dad's sickness made schooling extremely difficult. The family fortune was depleted, older siblings flung far seeking survival, while Jose was stuck looking after his old man with stipends from menial jobs he could garner locally.

His dream of becoming an electrical engineer looked too late and almost impossible when Jose finally had a little glimpse of a chance at age twenty-eight. A city firm recruited apprentices in the community, and Jose was given the humble role of a technical attendant. He was partnered with the senior engineer working on a major food processing project in the firm. With the stint of hard work, reliability, and utter dedication, he served the company almost day and night for ten full years. The stipend he was getting initially went toward the rent for his humble accommodation and the basics, yet he looked happy and full of life every day at work.

Getting to work one morning he found his boss worried and unhappy, the assistant engineer in the research department had been poached by a similar company. The fear of losing the exclusive knowledge of the invention to another company was palpable in the firm in the days to come. A new assistant had to be recruited, but the boss was not ready to expose himself and the invention again. Jose was considered for the job, but his boss assumed that he lacked the prerequisite knowledge for the role. While this musing was going on, the boss realised that there was no gap or lagging behind in the daily routine for two weeks. Curiosity made him realize that even though Jose had not been formally trained as an engineer, he had taken a keen interest in the research routine, learned sufficiently from the departed assistant, and had been reading the relevant materials for the past two years on the advice of the departed assistant.

The boss was impressed and recommended him for the job and formal training as an engineer at the nearby university while on the job. Time flew by, and he graduated as an engineer with second class upper and wealth of experience at the age of forty-two. The project had been completed, and the firm had received a patent. Jose's name came up as part of the contributors to the development, courtesy of the goodwill and kind heart of his boss. He was given one percent of the ownership, which he received with gladness, not knowing that commercial success was looming in the corner. The market success of the invention beat everyone hollow. Jose's one percent share made him a very rich, *resourceful, and happy electrical engineer with a family of his own in his mid-forties. He exceeded his ambitions and arrived grander than he had dreamed despite the fact that he got out of the block late and his path was assailed with dream-killing difficulties. Jose attributed his amazing trajectory to a decision he had made to himself at the beginning of his ordeal. He had decided to nurture positive energy within and run the uncharted race of unknown ahead of him with same. It paid off.*

Lesson # 10 – Take choice seriously, and very seriously.

Chose Progress Over Retrogression

In the concept of living, energy is a major vital force that determines the motions of life. We live in a result-oriented world. The living cannot be pretentious about our relentless crave and hot desire for results. Newton's second law of motion is applicable in many life scenarios: alluding to the fact that motion recorded is a function of how much positive energy is applied to the mass. Jose had a choice of retrogression at various junctions of the journey above.

- He could have not dreamt of becoming an engineer in the first place.
- He could have gotten used to the community cocoon and not ventured out after being stuck that long.
- He could have focussed on the job as a mere means to earn salary and not an opportunity to learn and imbibe skills.
- The stress of combining university education with the assistant job when he was offered could have made him plead only for the job.

He rather chose the only sensible way, which was to forge ahead no matter how long it took him to take off. An athlete who abandons the race because others got out of the block ahead at the sound of the gun is considered unsportsmanlike, unserious, and negative.

Arrival in Spite of Disappointment

One of the most negative energies you will deal with is the negative energy of disappointment. Nothing drains our drive to forge on more than disappointment. It drains off all the enthusiasm and makes effort investment a waste time. You will unavoidably have to deal with disappointment in your life at some point.

- Disappointment with yourself for not meeting some standard you expect of yourself.
- Disappointed when the support structures and systems around you fail to hold you up or meet your needs.
- Disappointment when your set expectations of situations are not met.
- Disappointment when your expectations of people are not met.
- Disappointment when life in an area or in general refuses to turn up as dreamt or planned.

Know for certain that one major aim of disappointment is to deplete the quantum of positive energy and aggregate negative energy within you. Time and timing can turn out to be assets or liabilities in the art of running life's race. Time and timing can become platforms of aggregating positive energy to forge on or negative energy to give up. How you interpret time and timing of life is significant in the kind of charge you place on the energy within you: positive or negative.

Lesson #11
- Late start doesn't necessarily mean late arrival

21

We live in a fast-paced world. Everything is quick, and time obviously does not wait for anyone. If you find yourself setting out later than you plan or later than your contemporaries, do not let this place a negative charge of discouragement and apathy on the drive within you.

Lesson #12
- Late start doesn't necessarily mean no arrival

* Van Gogh was said to have not started painting until his late twenties, and most of the great paintings were painted in the last two tears of his life. Certain circumstances of life are simply beyond your control. You may find yourself wrestling with a late start as a result. Some circumstances that are within your control might have slipped out of your hand, thereby leaving you lagging behind. Whatever the circumstances for your late start, it must not be the pre-occupation of your mind or you will lose a great deal of positive energy and aggregate so much negative energy to quit all together. Your focus must be on starting anyway and arriving somehow.

Lesson #13
- No start certainly means no arrival

The greatest disservice you can do yourself is to clock yourself out of starting. Don't do it no matter how far behind you are in time and achievement. If you focus on those who had early start and seeming early arrival around you, you will aggregate a very lethargic negative energy of inferiority, apathy, and a "what's the point starting this late "attitude. Whereas the truth is that life is kind of cyclic in its presentation of opportunity. Your mates may have gone with the early cycles and probably enjoy or even flaunt the fruits of arrival right before your eyes. Do not spiral into believing that all good cycles have been taken; early cycles aren't the only good cycle. Late cycles, too, have their places and can bring lasting fulfilment and happiness. Focus on the goal and aggregate the positive energy to start late if you have to. Arrival time is a count down only from starting.

Enthused and not Disappointed
Enthusiasm is a priceless gem of positive energy needed within by every achiever. The world is not out there to encourage you, mind you. The world is out there watching whether you truly mean it when you vow to be happy and successful. Many spanners thrown at the wheel are not to create sound but to stop the spinning. Many of the challenges you are dealing with are aimed to sap up the force of enthusiasm within you and kill the flickers and flames of excitement you possess.

One of the discoveries you will come into is the fact that not everything that excites and drives you will excite and drive others around you, not even your best mate. It is your own positive energy; keep it alive.

** Abraham Lincoln was not a politician initially but a business man. He suddenly developed enthusiasm for politics to the non-admiration of his peers, and he made a good deal out of it and became the 16th president of the United States of America. Sustenance of the union and abolition of the salve trade were milestones in the American political landscape. Both were Lincoln's legacy.

The fire of desire, drive to get on, passion to live well, urge to get the job done, and all similar enthusiasm for progress are the positive energy you must cultivate, retain, and renew in daily living.

23

Surmount but not Conquered

If you live long enough, you will come across challenges that seem to defile all solutions. Troubles that refuse to leave and mountains that refuse to move. Such challenges seem determined and designed to defy and ultimately break you; This is called crisis. The sole body language of the crisis will be to let you know that you are ordinary, conquerable, and not as untouchable, smart, or strong as you think you are. Such crisis may come as a health challenge, financial, relational, career or other form of very close-quarter troubles.

We talk of surmounting a mountain, but now it seems the mountain is the one surmounting you. That's fine – just don't get conquered. How should I not get conquered when I have been surmounted in this and that other area of my life? I am sure this is a question that you actually expect me to answer. Life can never be summarised as a single thing or by a single experience. Life is made of up very many things that come together and happen over time. Do not surrender any aspect of life to crisis without fighting hard for it. If you lose a part to the crisis, do not lump in the other aspects that are intact for the crisis to take as spoils of war. You may have lost one aspect. Keep the remaining and enjoy them as much as you can.

The sad thing about negative energy is that it will try to deny you the opportunity of enjoying the remaining cake called life simply because a part was broken off. Stop saying nothing remains. Face what remains and eat it. You may find out that you can be filled and be satisfied with what is left after all.

* From general information available on the subject.
** From general information available on the subject.

ENERGY RECOGNITION

ENERGY RECOGNITION

Lesson #14 – Anticipate but don't assume effects.

Not Every Energy Will Build You

The parable of life is that you were born a little baby and expected to be built in the course of living to a fully-grown adult. All your faculties and organs were given to you in tiny miniature form at birth. They evolve as you imbibe energy and nutrients in various forms and at various stages of growth.

Life expectation is for all babies to ultimately become adults, save any tragedy.

Positive energy will build you towards your expectations of life. There are scales and linear measurements in clinics and hospital to measure growth per time when babies are brought in for check-ups. This is to ascertain that the desired effect is being realised from what the babies are exposed to as nutrients. In like manner, you need to weigh and measure certain dimensions and parameters in life to gauge the positivity or negativity of the energy you mostly engage.

Positive Energy Is Needed for Happiness

Happiness is a universal currency and a global citizen. Everybody wants to be happy. Truth is, everybody has the universal right to be happy. Except for despots, sadists, and psychopaths, happiness is always derived from positive happenings. People who find happiness in a negative happening must have built up enormous negative energy over a period of time till they become twisted and freaks of nature. The same goes for those who find happiness in the right thing and the right way, they must have configured themselves over time to find happiness the right way. You must congregate positive energy within yourself over time. It is better to be happy than sad. It is also much better to find happiness the right way and doing the right thing.

Positive Energy is Needed for Fulfilment

Fulfilment is the ultimate personal reward. It is the ultimate medal and prize in all the races we invest energy into in life. Peace, rest, and contentment are some of the final stops we aim for in the journey of life, and they all point at finding fulfilment. Fulfilment is close to but deeper than happiness. One can find happiness and miss fulfilment whereas one cannot find fulfilment and not find happiness. This underscores the importance of the methodology and means of finding happiness.

One can make money, have fun, achieve greatness, look happy, and be as hollow on the inside as an empty gas cylinder.

Attention has to be paid to what is built on the inside to achieve our goals on the outside. For instance, if you loathe yourself because you envy others, you may be well driven to achieve success but will still not find fulfilment even when you have more material success than them. You will be the unhappy boss in the big airy office who has everything and yet far less happy compared to the menial workers in a tiny corner down the street. When you find yourself high in the hierarchical order and low in the fulfilment scale, you need to reconfigure the energy driving you within. You need more of positive energy.

Positive Energy is Needed for Good Influence

The world we live in is as good as the dominant forces of influence bore on it over time. Leaders, inventors, fellow community dwellers, family, and indeed almost everyone within our sphere of existence ultimately create some kind of influence in our world one way or another. The influence can be significant or negligible.

The world we live in and the kind of life we live are all products of influence. Some set of people influenced me to think that I could type my ideas and design the pages on a computer to create a book. The inventors encouraged me to make the use of the computer to that effect by the way of users friendly inventions.. Me being influenced to use the machine in that way was probably the deliberate intention of the designers or it may not be, but an influence has been created knowingly or unknowingly.

What you need to know is that you are creating both intended and non-intended influence in all you do. Some you can help and some are outside of your control. Quantum tunnelling and subsequently nuclear fusion were an innocent discovery of research into particle behaviour with an unintended influence of creating the now notorious and much feared nuclear warfare.

You can measure and tag the energy you are accumulating inside and utilising on the outside by the intended and unintended influence it generates. Positive energy ultimately brings common good.

Lesson #15
- Certain energy burn than they build.

Whereas positive energy builds you towards your goal, brings happiness, brings fulfilment, and creates good influence. Negative energy will do the opposite.
- It will burn you away from your goal.
- It will rob you of happiness that drives.
- It will deny you fulfilment.
- It will create negative influence on your behalf in whatever sphere you are operating in.

The burning will always start within you and your aura before it starts burning down things on the outside all around and beyond you. Think of what great damage can be done by hatred, self-loathing, envy, greed, intolerance, wrath, and the likes.

Negativity Always Looking for Initiates
Our world is rich in men and women who have taken time to accumulate, invent, or develop enormous venom of negative energy. They literally look for who to dump it on. When you meet them at the train station, bus stop, on the queue, in the office or worse still at home, all they do is to release vials of poison into your aura for you to battle with all day long or even longer.

The irony is that most of them don't even know how dark and how poisonous the negative energy they emit is. But the reality is that they are looking for who to initiate into the negativity club, knowingly or unknowingly.

Your job is to avoid the dump. Learn to clean it up, and don't let it stay on you if it has been rubbed on you. Negative attitude and characteristics aren't genetic, but they can get passed down the familial line. It's a rub-on.

It can be rubbed on from a boss to the whole office and within an entire community. Negative energy can spread like bugs from friend to friend and among associates. It is always looking for someone to initiate into carrying it and passing it on — it's your responsibility to decline this unprofitable offer.

Lesson #16
- Classify it for what it is.

Your job is to call a spade what it is and classify the energy you have accumulated as the predominant driving force within you.

Redemption of the right energy within your aura and beginning of progress start when you correctly classify the energy you mostly operate in. It is your decision to exercise in personal adjustment to achieve your desired change. Proper classification will help you decide on dissipation or aggregation of the energy, depending on what charge it carries. Feeling bad about yourself and being angry or frustrated with the unappealing results you get are both self-defeating, rather, try to classify the driving force on the inside, this is what ultimately translates to progress on the outside.

Having done that, start your journey to the happy life you desire with the next chapters that start with *positive energy discovery.*

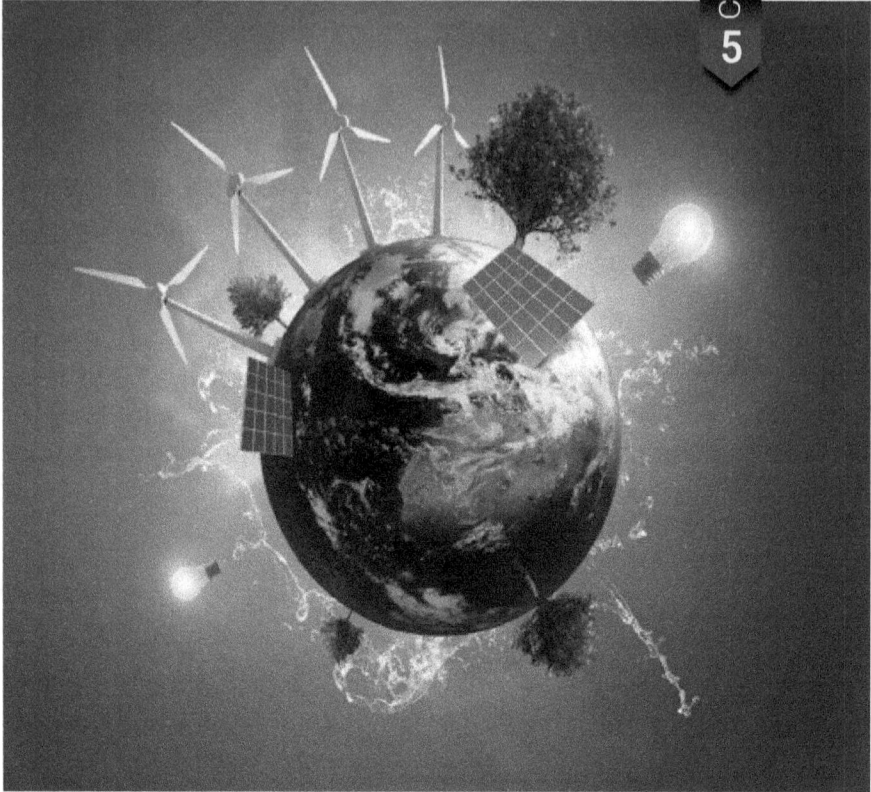

THE RIGHT ENERGY DISCOVERY

Chapter Five

THE RIGHT ENERGY DISCOVERY

What Works for You and Makes You Tick

Everyone's purpose is wired into his or her inner configuration. There is something that makes for smooth operation even in rough terrain within a man or woman of purpose. There is a solid part of you that is fundamental and does not give in to the rough terrain of the outside easily. Your utmost productivity, moral fibres, and values are derived from and attached to and reside here. Character is built around this spot of positive energy. This is a spot that has to be discovered by you, as it defines your ultimate results and character.

It makes the difference between:

- Holding on under pressure or breaking into pieces at the slightest press and push.

- Finding a way out of dark tunnels of life by all means or staying in the dark cloud of sadness and depression till the end.

- Fighting on in spite of failure or giving up at the first appearance of failure and difficulties.

- Taking responsibility in the face of difficulties or blaming others and luck for life's outcome.

- Attracting the right people and the right platform for needed progress or repelling and being resistant to help and needed assistance.
- Breaking new ground in spite of the previous success or taking premature rest and fizzling out even when there are much more that can still be achieved.

Not Just What Feels Good

Feeling is fleeting as they say and can oscillate easily with time and terrain. For example, food makes you feel good when you are hungry and have an appetite. Same food can become a repulsive burden that makes you feel sick when you are filled up or lacking in appetite. Irrespective of the feeling it elicits, the unchangeable fact is that food is needed for survival. You therefore cannot make a permeant decision about its consumption based on transient feelings.

Positive energy is not just about what makes you feel good for the moment, but the overall effect it bears on your person. Many addicts move from the "feel good"phase to the addictive phase while mistaking the feel good for positive energy.

You must not narrow life to the feel good alone or negative energy will mask itself with temporary good feelings and hide its destructive part till you have consumed enough and the devastating effects will start to show.

Think of a medicine that is very bitter or unpleasant in   taste, it is often coated with sweetener for the patients to swallow. Most destructive habits with negative energy are coated in sweetener of good feelings. Watch out for what you take in!

What Really Counts

Tesher and Shivat were upwardly mobile professionals of similar abilities, qualifications, and ambitions working for the city's leading PR firm with a global network of clientele. They were team leaders in major projects especially at events, which required working with the clients on outpost locations.

The high-end nature of the firm made the working environment seriously demanding and loaded with enormous work place pressure.

Shivat joined the organisation before Tesher and so had a bit more experience than Tesher. Their boss was the king of PR industry. He was well connected, quite impulsive, and extremely demanding.

There was no overtime as the work had to be done, dusted, and delivered in any case. The foremost motivation for the team was the satisfaction of seeing clients' mandate delivered to the letter. This unwritten demand on self for delivery kept the firm on the high end of the PR industry over the years.

Along with this came the benefit of good remuneration and welfare package with huge exposure to the high end of the PR industry. It was always a utopian experience for anyone privileged to join the firm in-spite of the underlying pressure and demands of the job.

Shivat soon stopped seeing all the opportunities and exposure as privileges, which they were. She started seeing such as rights and sometimes as a burden. Tolerance for the long hours and other demands on the job started waning which began to show negatively in her demeanour towards the team and more importantly towards clients. In no time, she started picking unnecessary and somewhat toxic arguments with colleagues, superiors, and even clients. The boss hated losing her with her wealth of experience and so put up with her in-spite of what was becoming a persistently, unpleasant manner.

The biggest event for the firm and the most demanding in preparation time and energy was for a particular client dealing in global leadership. The two weeks event was regarded as the biggest and most extensive in scale and scope in their annual calender. Nobody was allowed leave, except for sickness or pre-booked maternity, during this period. Shivat against this background made herself unavailable for some days or was a no-show even when she was present.

This pressure equilibrium was shifted to Tesher who did her best to salvage an excellent delivery that could not be faulted but rather raise the company's profile.

A year later, the huge client referred to above absorbed the PR firm into its global group. The merger made Tesher's boss so much richer as the minority shareholder in the merger. The regional king of PR had just taken a global forward leap in the real business sense.

The client had invited the PR boss and his team leaders to a dinner a week after the aforementioned annual event to shoe appreciation and test the water of possible acquisition which ultimately led to the merger with the boss. It was more or less a stake holders get-together from the look of things, with a handful of employees invited, who were not involved in nor invited to the caucuses and small group talks in the course of the long night.

The positive aura Tesher carried in delivering her lines at the event, which she also brought to the dinner, did not escape the big client and a gentleman in particular. He ultimately struck a conversation with her and noticed in her not just a great worker but a reliable hand who would not dampen the boardroom up with toxicity if given the access. The gentleman happened to be the chairman in waiting for the global leadership group. He had been at the event as part of the many years of on-ground observation required of him before taking over the reign.

Shivat and Tesher were nominated by their boss for one to be chosen by the board of the bigger firm as the representative of their minority stake in the merger. Whosoever is chosen will have the oversight of the operation for the PR division in the merger. It was a straight forward decision for the new chairman and the board to gravitate toward Tesher as the preferred one.

Few years down the lane, Tesher was called up to join the board of the group of company to bear the impact of her positivity on the entire global operation. She was not just rewarded for being a hard worker with deep sense of commitment, she was singled out for her attitude of positivity

Lesson #17
- What you bring to the table can be great, but how you bring it makes the ultimate difference.

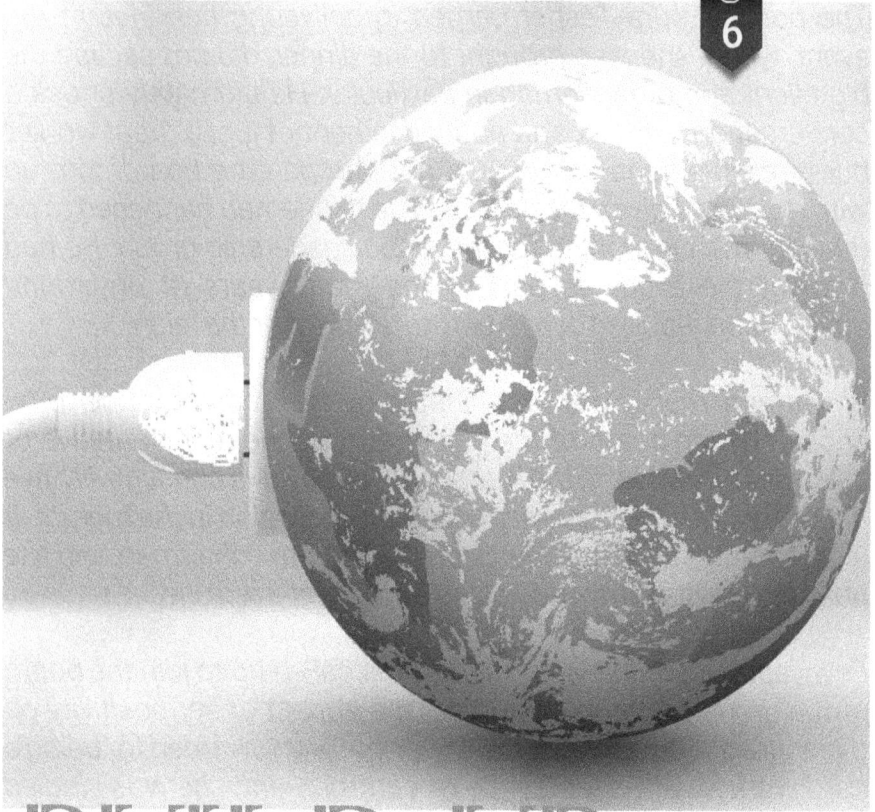

BUILD UP
ENERGY

Chapter Six

BUILD UP ENERGY

Time Demand for Positive Energy
Every good thing in our world was built over time. Building up a good aura of positive energy within and around yourself takes time.

- *It takes time to recognise where to work on yourself.*
- *It may take time to even realize you need to work on yourself.*
- *It will definitely take time for the work to kick in.*
- *It takes time to start erasing the negative energy and clean up the dark cloud it has brought on you.*
- *It takes time to get used to shutting down the old negativity as it comes back to try and dominate you again.*
- *You need time to recover and keep doing the needful when you find yourself falling short of your desired positive energy level.*

It is important to know that you need devotion and not a glossing over to get there. In the same light, do not be too hard on yourself, as Rome was not built in a day.

One thing you must never do with time is to waste it on or around negativity. Use your lifetime to move against it.

Attitude Demand for Positive Energy

High intelligence quotient (IQ) is far from what it takes in life to be happy and find fulfilment. Emotional quotient (EQ) has a lot to do with the aura that comes from people, and nobody loves bad aura. This is where the whole concept of attitude and body language comes in.

Many talented sport stars have come under hard and sometimes unfair scrutiny from fans for failing to lift their team out of defeat or to victory in crucial games when such is much needed. It is not always for lack of skill and even effort or will to win but from the demeanour with which the skills and efforts were brought to the game. Nothing on the outside reflects the internal desire to get the job done, and so the effort is neither seen nor appreciated.

More battles have been won or lost to attitude than to weapons and numbers in ancient and modern warfare.

Look after Yourself

Every human by instinct was born to look after him/herself. It is your responsibility to look after yourself, and part of looking after yourself is to recognise the flip side of self that precipitates *negative energy* against the self you ought to look after.

Chief among what you need to deal with in looking after yourself are *self-defeat*, *self-pity*, and *selfishness*. I promise you that they are very attractive and appealing at one point or another to every one of us, but they are killers of drive and evolvement. These three are not good masters, neither are they profitable servants. They are so cruel that they will set you on journey of no discovery and incur loss with no recovery if you follow them or

they follow you far enough.
Self-defeat, self-pity, and selfishness can:
- *Make you keep looking in vain for what you already have.*
- *Make you lose what is vital for what is inconsequential.*
- *Make you devalue what you are given.*
- *Make you detest what you possess.*
- *Make you desperately desire what you will never get.*
- *Make you forcibly take what will do you no good.*
- *Make you wrongfully take what can do you harm.*
- *Make victims of all around you.*
- *Make you the ultimate victim of everyone.*

Work on Yourself
Good and winning attitudes are not just talent or mere gifts hat just perch on people like a bird on a tree effortlessly, they are products of self-imposed demand to come across in the right and proper way as often as you can.

The concept of positive energy, as mentioned earlier on, is not about perfection. It is not about not having negative thoughts or even being caught up with occasional negativity. It is about not allowing negativity to become your default. You will encounter many failures on your journey of self-imposed, self-improvement, but working on self is worth the pain. You will come out refined and of more value on the other side of the furnace.

One major mountain that breeds negative attitude is the mountain of self.

Self can poison your well of energy if not well managed. The mere fact that life demands you to look after yourself makes swinging onto the wrong side of self an easy possibility.

Lesson #18- Work more on balance up when working on yourself:

Here are ten quick lessons on self-balacing you need to take on board .

1. *Don't neglect **yourself**; nobody else will look after you.*
2. *Don't be too absorbed with **yourself**, or you will start irritating people.*
3. *Don't force **yourself** on others, or everyone will start avoiding you.*
4. *Don't make **yourself** available to everyone, or some will start using you wrongly.*
5. *Don't make life all about **yourself**, or you will be destructive and hurt people.*
6. *Don't spare **yourself** of needed adjustment, or you will not grow.*
7. *Don't deny **yourself** the requisite sacrifices for improvement, or you will not evolve.*
8. *Don't self-destruct; it is the greatest injustice you can do to **yourself**.*
9. *Don't make **yourself** unserious, or you won't be taken seriously.*
10. *Don't take **yourself** too seriously, or you will mistake yourself as the only building block of humanity puzzle.*

Energy Trimming
When the energy level is swinging, take a break. Sit back and do a self-appraisal. Nobody can appraise you better than you.

Others may taint their appraisals of you with love, hatred, likeness, dislike, or even prejudice.

Unlike the academic examination that is set and marked by someone else, life's examinations are ultimately set and marked by oneself.
Happiness, fulfilment, and even success is ultimately self-appraised. Others may be clapping for someone while the one being clapped for is mourning in the inside. Many things you can fake to others that you cannot fake to yourself

You are the pilot of your life. All the data are set before you so you can know where and what to trim for a great flight and good landing.

Part of trimming is to make a U-turn from an energy path. It could mean making a few corrections here and there. You were born blank so that you can appreciate change and learning. The language you speak, the way you think, and virtually everything you do as adult were not born with you. You learned them as you grew. You can learn and unlearn anything in your energy-trimming process.

Stake Holder Energy
Don't live your life as if, if it falls apart, you won't be the one bearing the brunt of it. Often, we live life as if we are doing it as favour for those who care about us. I have seen grown-up and children handling life as if they are doing it in proxy for their parents. Not at all. If it falls apart, you will be the first and foremost victim thereof. If you lose your job, your partner or colleague won't be the jobless one, it will be you no longer earning.

Lesson #19 – Bring your A-game where nothing else can win.

- *Live your life as if you are the sole stakeholder who has all to gain.*
- *Make it a mandate to bring on all it takes to make it work out well.*
- *Owe it to yourself to do your job as a stakeholder who will find joy and fulfilment if it works out well.*

Gratitude Over Entitlement
Gratitude is beyond saying thank you to someone. It shows in the attitude.

Shivat got used to good things happening around her and took them for granted. She got used to being accepted the way she was till she became unacceptable for something better. She got used to being relevant at the level she was till she lost relevance for the next level.

If you have travelled the world a bit, you will be more circumspect in your entitlement mentality and become more grateful for the little things life affords you.

Do not just be grateful for yourself. Be grateful for others when you see good things happen to them. It is called being gracious and appreciative.

Gratitude creates a great bubble of positivity within you and an aura of good grace around you.

It opens up the spring of new reason and fountain of a new season for living. Gratitude can be sacrificial at times, especially

43

when there is more to be sad and complain about than there is to be grateful for.

Do it anyway for positive energy's sake.

Energy Deficit
Deficit in any transaction is the outstripping of generation by consumption. When what you consume is more than what you bring to the table, you create deficits for others to bear.

When others have to keep bearing the deficit you create, you soon become a liability. Whatever or whoever is creating an energy deficit for you is a sort of liability. It will bankrupt your energy deposit if adjustment is not insisted upon and sought with all intent. The best way out is to tilt the balance and adjust what is being brought to the table by each party. No desirable team member should create a perpetual increase in team time, energy, and budget for damage control.

- *Your first line of adjustment may be to reduce the quantum of energy you invest (rather waste) and conserve more.*
- *Your other line of action may be to stop being a recipient of the energy- sapping and strength-sucking negativity being brought to the table by whatever or whoever.*

Being a Plus Team Component
The essence of creating a team in whatever form, on whatever project, and of whatever proportion is to leverage on collective contribution. The aim is for each component to bring much more to the table than they take thereby creating a rich chest of asset.

When the liability you bring to the team is more than the asset you add to the team, a deficiency is created. Knowing fully well that a team can not thrive on deficiency, one major focus you must task yourself with is not to let your liability outstrip your asset creation for the team. Otherwise the team will either let you go, or you will kill the team someday.

Here are ten tips for being a plus team component:

i. *What you do in and for the team is very important, but how you do it is much more important.*
ii. *Your personal luggage must not occupy much of the team space.*
iii. *If it is all about you, a team is needless.*
iv. *Do not bankrupt the team of goodwill simply because you bring lots of goods to the team. Goods cannot pay for goodwill.*
v. *Do not bankrupt the team of goods simply because you bring some goodwill to the team. Bearer of good will needs to be sustained by goods.*
vi. *Moving the team forward is not same as rocking the team always. You can be creative without causing chaos.*
vii. *Energy for speed is compromised when much is needed for stability.*
viii. *The lifespan of a team is most likely longer than that of each component.*
ix. *Don't make maximum withdraw in your goodwill credit. Ignominy is the next offer after that.*
x. *Work hard on balance; standing long requires two legs.*

Lesson #20
- Make enough sacrifice to build the most positive energy for the game and your life. It will give you the edge and push you ahead in the game and life.

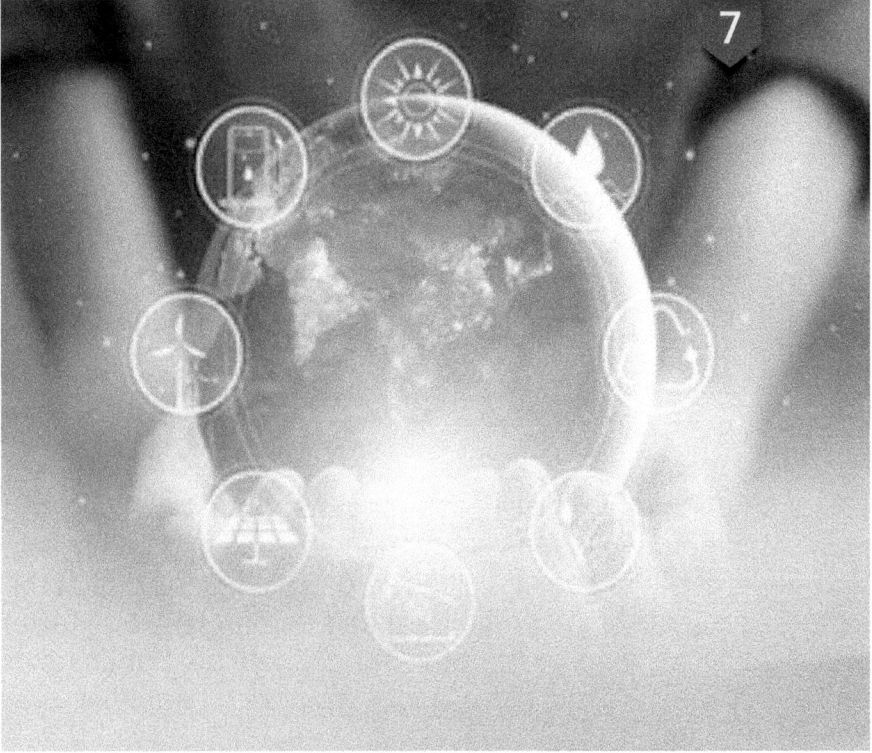

GENERATE MORE

Chapter Seven

GENERATE MORE

You May Need A Lot

Life is sapping in an energy context. The routine of living can look simple but is indeed very demanding. Visiting the streets and alleys of our towns and cities across the world point at the simple fact that living can be hard and demanding. Life takes and saps a lot of energy from the living. There are hundreds of millions of sad, broken, bitter, angry, frustrated people all over the place and yet:

- *Nobody was born sad; we became sad.*
- *Nobody was born bitter; we became bitter.*
- *Nobody was born broken; we became broken.*
- *Nobody was born angry; we became angry.*
- *Nobody was born frustrated; we became frustrated.*

Lesson # 21 – Time allows things to happen, good or bad.

Take Charge of Your Destiny

The stark reality of the energy demand of life must spur you into the resolve of never finding yourself in a positive energy deficit again. Whether you are ready to give it or not, life will demand energy from you. The wise thing to do is to be ready to give it whatever it takes.

Your destiny is yours to fulfil, to keep, and to preserve.

Events of life will unfold, and many will come upon you like billows, with their attending effects. Never yield your positive energy ground to any of them. People will hurt you. Life will treat you real bad. Do not hand over your positive energy. It is your insurance for sanity and progress, keep it.

Even when your loved ones rally around you to help you work it out, you need to know that life will at some point not take a donation of energy from others on your behalf. It wants you to be on the spot, fighting the battle and generating the energy. Whether you borrow it from others, it does not matter as long as it is generated in you.

Have you come across someone that everyone is trying to help stand up in life and they prop the person up but the feet have no strength to stand upon, and so they had to stop. So it is when all we do is rely on other people's energy to prop up us in life and blame them when we can't stand much less move forward.

If you want to make progress, energy is demanded of you. You need to stop being excessively reliant. Start generating your own motion.

Responsibility is Right Response
Life is not black and white; there are many unfair grey areas to life. Grey areas sometimes evade answer.

Questions and answers of why are not always the right response to some energy-sapping questions of life; having the right response is always the answer.

Lesson # 22 – There can always be an alternate response to every question of life.

- Instead of "why me" – the right response can be- now that it's me, I will have to do something about it.
- Instead of "how bad" I have sunk – the response can be that I will come out good.
- Instead of "how long" do I have to – the response can be that I will make the most of my time here.
- Instead of "whose fault" – the response can be, not again.

The list can be endless, but the energy to find the right response no matter the demand is what you need to take responsibility for.

Many questions of life pop up like computer cookies with viruses. They are out to crash your system and make you aggregate loads of negativity, as they are mostly rhetoric with their negative answer lurking somewhere in the corner of your head to affirm negativity.

Take it upon yourself to find alternate answer.

One of the legend of the east has it that Zabej was a mythical man of great nobility. He was the most successful and the happiest of his whole clan at the end of his life, but it was not so at the onset. There were many questions raised on the need to have another child when his mother was pregnant with him after nine others. Their misgiving and myth around his birth were escalated when he was born sickly and the family fortune dwindled greatly a few years down the line. All his brothers learned a trade, but he was not even considered as fit and good enough for any enterprise.

As he grew up, question of why he was being treated differently in not a pleasant way arose in his mind, and so he decided to consult the solution parchments. Legends has it that the practice in those day was to consult the parchment left behind by the patriarch of the clan whenever one was confused about life; and lo the answer would be there staring you in the face as you read.

The first huddle for Zabej was to learn lettering and symbolism of the ancients with which the solution parchments were coded. He spent the bulk of his years doing this till he became an expert in lettering, numbering, code cracking, and symbolism.

Instead of Zabej finding an answer to the question of why he was so not reckoned with for success, he rather found a trade in the course of time. Everyone in the clan and beyond who needed urgent answers from the parchments of solution soon started contracting him till he had a long waiting list. He became so busy and sought after by a very long list of clienteles, including kings and nobles, till the parchment house became his official postcode (zip).

Charges and rewards soon made him so rich till he became richer than everyone in the clan. Relevance and positive impacts made him so happy and fulfilled that he had forgotten what led him to parchment searching in the first place. He only remembered a century later when a young man who attempted suicide was brought to him and he asked the boy what the problem was, and the young lad said he felt unfortunate, unloved and unwanted by his family and clan. .

Lesson #23

- Good mental aptitude is enhanced by serious mental exercise. Use your brain to carve a path. That's why it was given.

EXPLORE
MORE

Chapter Eight

EXPLORE MORE

From Probable to Possible.

Nothing is certain in itself until someone removes the negativity of impossible in the probability and harnesses the positivity therein. If all the fears and misgivings that stop us from making progress had mouth and could tell us that they really don't have the power to stop or hurt us, we would almost all be great achievers in life. Alas, they don't. You are the one with mouth. You are the one who must tell your fear and misgiving that you won't be stopped any longer and in any case.

Fear Must Make You Do Something

Life is configured for the dwellers to be found doing something. If all the sicknesses and diseases can tell us that they won't kill us or hurt us any further, science would suffer a great negligence. The fear of death and hurt from sicknesses and diseases have greatly helped us create many ground-breaking medical solutions with many still to come. The same is applicable to development in every other sector of human endeavour.

Lesson #24 - Fear feels paralysing, but it can and it is meant to make us do something.

- *If you fear being poor, do something to be rich.*
- *If you fear being sick, do all you can to stay healthy.*
- *If you fear rejection, be acceptable.*
- *If you not being suffering in silence, speak out loud.*
- *If you fear loneliness, learn to stop scaring people away.*
- *If you fear the carnage of war, make way for peace to happen.*
- *If you fear failure, pursue success at all cost.*

Most of the great inventions and innovations we enjoy today came about when men and women of goodwill were stared in the face by the fear of humanity losing out if those innovations and inventions didn't happen.

Losing time and goods to the peril of sea crossing motivated the invention of the flying machine, and so today we fly in aircrafts.

Stop Saying I Can't
Negativity has voices, and one major voice of negativity is the voice of "I can't" when indeed you can.

- I can't start all over again – *Truth is, yes, you can and still make up for the losses by starting all over again.*
- I can't make it - *Of course, you can make it. Those who make it aren't alien or super human.*
- I can't find happiness again - *Your feeling is energy driven. You can change the direction with the right energy.*
- I can't go through it again – *If you have to, please do it. Going through it again may be progress in disguise.*
- I can't emerge from this – *You were not born to sink;*

hence you live on the surface of the ground and not in a tunnel. You will always find your level.

- I can't catch up – *Probably you do not need to catch up. You may just need to keep ploughing through, and you will arrive at your destination after all.*
- I can't do better – *The current version of yourself is the old version. There is always a new version hidden somewhere. Yes, you can do better.*
- I can't recover– *Recovery is a process. It does not discriminate, if allowed to take place and have its course.*

Probably you have this funny feeling that stretching yourself some more for the desired positivity will hurt you. Well, you don't have to and you are not meant to get hurt by change. You are just asked to exert yourself and stretch a little more for greater possibility. Sometimes, the demand to improve your input sounds like asking for your neck on the gallows. Don't succumb and fade away; just stretch a little more.

Create an Upset
In sports, when a small team or a lesser star defeats a bigger team or a well-known and well established star, it is referred to as an upset.
It is common football, snooker, boxing, and other sports. When this happens, for example in a long tennis match, the interviewer will always push to know the state of mind of the player who created the upset.

In almost all cases, such players will foremost acknowledge the unfavourable disparity in the ability, experience, and star power of himself/herself and the opponent. Following closely will be the fact that he/she just decided to give himself/herself a

55

chance in the match, and hence the upset was created. You may not be a match in strength and capacity to your challenge, but you can give yourself the chance of victory and happiness, who knows what may give way for your progress in the process.

Make the Fraction Whole

In mathematics, we can get a whole number from a fraction by simply adding a complementary fraction. In like manner, uncertainties and probabilities in life can be converted to wholesome certainty if we seek out the complementary fractions. We can also take away some fractions from another to get a whole figure.

Happy and fulfilled people do not just wake up and find themselves happy and neither do the sad ones. What happens is mostly mathematical. You may not just be happy by chance. You may have to seek out the missing fractions that will complement the fractions you are carrying around before happiness will happen. Rest assured that there are fractions that can be added to or taken from the one you already have to make a whole figure of success, happiness and fulfilment you so much desire.

The fractions in your hands are your chances, even when they do not look whole like what you really want; do not throw them away in frustrations and anger; neither seek the fractions someone else is carrying, they may not complement yours.

You cannot be closed up to addition and subtraction in life and be truly whole and happy. Part of your positive energy exercise is explorations of adding and subtracting from that which you already possess in order to create the perfect wholeness you seek. Negative energy will push you to throw away fractional platforms and chances in anger and frustration simply because they do not look or feel whole enough to meet your requirement for happiness. Whereas, positive energy lays the demand and responsibility on you to make most of such platforms and chances while seeking what to add or take away from them to make them whole. You may have to add more skill, more friendship, more education, more time and so on. In like manner you may have to take off some.

Hanging In There

Quitting is almost the greatest injustices you can do to yourself in the game of life.

In sports, many teams and individuals have come back from the brink of defeat and created another kind of upset simply by hanging on. After the game, the most common question is how they pulled it off even when it looked like all was lost and the game was over.

The answer is always that they stayed around in the heat of it. "We just hung in there".

Once you entertain the thought of quitting too much, your positive energy level will nose dive, giving way to the negative energy of guilt, self-pity, regret, frustration, and ultimate full stop.

Lesson #25 - Best certainty in life may start with the worst probability. Give yourself a chance.

TRANSFORM IT

Chapter Nine

TRANSFORM IT

One of the major scientific laws of energy says that energy can neither be created nor destroyed but can be transformed from one form to another. This is called the first law or the law of conservation of energy. To a high degree of reality, this applies to positive and negative energy of life too.

The ability to tamper with what nature gives in order to get it to work for us is a major privilege for humanity. Whatever quantum or charge of energy is thrown at you by nature can be transformed to what you need and what works for you.

* *Rosa Parks* (1913-2005) of Montgomery, Alabama, United States, the iconic woman referred as the first lady of civil right was an introvert. Nevertheless, she was famed for refusing to give up her seat in the dark days of segregation in the US. The event highlighted the ongoing racial injustice in public transportation, among other platforms. Her protest and subsequent arrest that day led to a mass boycott of public transport in Montgomery. The cascade of events from that moment of speaking up by an introvert ultimately led to the

change in segregation rules on public transport in that part of the world forever.

What Do You want?
It is inherent in every human to want happiness, joy, fulfilment, and a good life in general. You are entitled to all of these and much more, but the sad reality of life is that you may not have been given what you want.
- *You may have to create an upset against all odds.*
- *You may have to give yourself an unusual chance in the face of denial.*
- *You may have to hang on for longer than usual.*

What You are Given
What we are given as human in birth, race, nationality, geographical location, lineage, family heritage, and all other odds of life are most definitely not same and equal. Yet we are all entitled as human with equal humanity to our different goals, aspirations, happiness, and fulfilment.

It takes a lot of positive energy to deal with what you are dealt not by choice and still bring home what you want as choice in life. Just like the transformation of energy to what is needed rather than becoming the victim of what is given and what is not given.

You Need to Work on Your Chance
The ultimate chance in life is the one you give yourself. You can move the mountain, crack the code, and ride the waves if you will give yourself a bit more of chance.

Good luck is the undue chance given to an individual, and we all won't have it in equal measure. For some it's plentiful, for others it is almost non-existent, they sadly tend to often experience bad luck.

The presence or absence of good luck or undue chance is not the ultimate determinant of life's outcome. The energy generated by them is the decider. Good luck with sufficient negativity will bring frustration and failure, while not so good luck with much positivity will create some upset that will bring success and happiness..

When You Are Given a Whole Chance
On occasions, you may be given whole chance with all its attending certainties void of probability. Your positive energy is `to transform such whole chance to un-missable opportunity to be fully harnessed. Make the most of it.

You are reading my book now and will likely recommend it to someone else and so on till it reaches the end of the earth. But the reality is that I gave myself the ultimate chance by writing it. The chance of being able to read, write, and think along the paradigm this book depicts is a chance I was given. The positive energy of bringing all of those together and bearing the whole weight of personal responsibility on making the book happen is mine to bring to the table.

On few occasions and in few avenues in your lifetime will you be given whole chance. Take responsibility. Avoid negative energy of wasting chances, ruining opportunities and being irresponsible.

When You Are Given Half a Chance
By half chance we mean literally half or any other fraction that is short of a whole chance. We are talking about insignificant chances, small chances, and all that are short of your expectations in chances.

- The first thing is to avoid the negative energy of despising your little chance and comparing it to your neighbour's whole chance, so to say. (It truly may not be as whole as it seems across the road after all). Your positive energy is to first and foremost focus on your fractional chance and not waste it on comparison, envy, frustration and anger.

- Whatever progress the little chance you have can accomplish, just do it. If the certificate you have can only get you enrolment for higher certificate that can ultimately get you a job, do it. If the little you are given is merely for survival, go ahead and survive first, flourish afterwards.

- Then start seeking how to add and multiply chances. The sad reality of existence is that opportunities seem always fair to the "have" and not the "have not." Hence the need for you to hold on with pride to that chance that you have in whatever shade or quantum. Hold it up for complementary chances to see and gravitate toward you. Most great sport and show-business stars were not born into greatness of any kind. They either had the fractional chance of passion, skill, or talent. Along the way came the other fractional chances of happenstance, relationship, mentoring, and the rest become history.

Lesson # 26
*- Make the most of your chance. It may be the only one for a long
 while.*

When You Are Given No Chance
In extreme cases of not being given an iota of a chance
whatsoever:
- You need to avoid the negative energy of bitterness as it
  will cloud your thinking and make you always see the
  remaining images of life in their inverted and upside
  forms.
- Your positive energy is to give yourself the chance you
  are denied by life and others.
- You must be determined that not only will you give
  yourself a chance but you will create the same chance
  denied you for others.
- Life takes a sweeter turn when you are not just living for
  yourself but see yourself as an addition to humanity with
  something positive to offer.
- Life chances may not always be served as a sizzling
  dinner in a golden plate on a set table with candle lights
  and basket of roses to match.
- You most likely will have to cook the meal of chance and
  serve yourself for now.
- If you thrive, you will be eventually served all the chances
  (*even the ones you don't need*) by the whole world later.
  You will have make the most of the little chance you have
  now in order to evolve and emerge from your little corner.

In reality, you may have to get the education by yourself, do the
apprenticeship, learn the trade, or source the capital. Your first
assignment in the difficult terrain of unemployment is to first

make yourself employable.

The positive energy of not being given a chance in life is that you don't have any fear of failure. You are being judged against zero. You can as well just pursue your non-existing chances with reckless abandon. You actually have nothing to lose when you are given no chance in the first place, so you can go all the way and risk the fall. You will be forgiven if you fail and revered if you succeed with no chance. But it will be sad if you do nothing.

Regret is a Game
The word regret can elicit either negative or positive energy in you, depending on how you play the game. I know many people do not want to hear the word regret as if it is entirely a negative thing. Regret is not a negative thing. It is a channel of improving your humanity if you handle it well. When you hear people saying they do not have any regret, it is not true. In fact, they have either dealt with it or are fighting one at that moment.

Regret Must Not be a Final Destination
Regret is a good experience if you do not make it your final destination. Regret will come when your target is missed or the consequences of your actions turn out badly. If you live long enough, you will have a few of them. You will do things wrong along the way. The consequences of some of them will make you feel sad and disappointed with yourself or your loved one. Forgive yourself and do not make that position of regret your final destination. Pitching your final tent on the ground of regret is like standing on corrosive. It will start to eat you up soon. You must move on no matter what. Many will want to help make it your final abode by reminding you and judging you with such failure. They are purveyors of negative energy. Run far away from them.

Create Positivity Even in Regret

The positive energy in regret lies in the fact that you hate to fail and disappoint, even though you did this time around. An indication that the shortcoming is not your default. It can be career failure, character failure, relational failure, or financial failure. The sense of regret shows that this is not your default. Regrets will help you improve your humanity if you handle them correctly.

- *Regret Can Generate Remorse* – Sane and normal human should feel bad for doing wrong, otherwise we will lose the essence of our humanity. Either by error or intent, wrong doings must generate remorse, which is a positive energy side of regret.
- *Regret Can Create Correction* – The essence of the positive energy of the remorse side of regret is for correction to be affected where and when possible. Your world may face the wrong direction and generate the very result you do not desire. At that point where you stop in regret, opportunity is being given to you to make correction and trim your path. Positive energy to make correction can be generated from the existing energy of regret.
- *Regret Can Encourage Learning* – Our world is an evolving one. Knowledge keeps increasing and our methodology keeps evolving. Only the static man suffers the regret of stagnation. Failure and disappointments can be indicators that more learning need be done. Most dominant winning teams in human fields of endeavour learn winning primarily from failure. Microsoft learned how to make Windows commercially successful with the 1986 edition after many failures. There is positive energy when regret leads to learning.

- *Regret Can Build up the Determination to Do It Right*– Regrets of failure and bad feelings that come with disappointment can spur positive energy of determination to get it right. In your lifetime, you will come across people who get it right in one attempt. They are few and far between, so do not wallow in regret of not being like such. Many successful people in one field or another are re-takers. They retook the course till they made it. Your positive energy from the regretful feeling of failure is to build up formidable determination that can not be withered down by anything. When you don't want to live in regret, you will give it not just your best shot; you will give it the needed shot till your desires are delivered.
- *Regret Can Makes You Circumspect* - One major positive energy to be derived from whatever cause regret is the lesson to learn to be circumspect. Not letting your guard down in a wrong way that makes you vulnerable. It is your positive energy that makes you cease being vulnerable. Life is full of predators, learning to keep your guard with circumspection is safety and must be part of lesson learned.

What Works

Your ultimate energy focus should be to move from what you want or what you are given to what will really work for you. This will help you to make most of what you are given and transform it to what you want ultimately.

Lesson #27 – Not everything is in its permanent state yet; you can work on it.

*From general information available on the subject

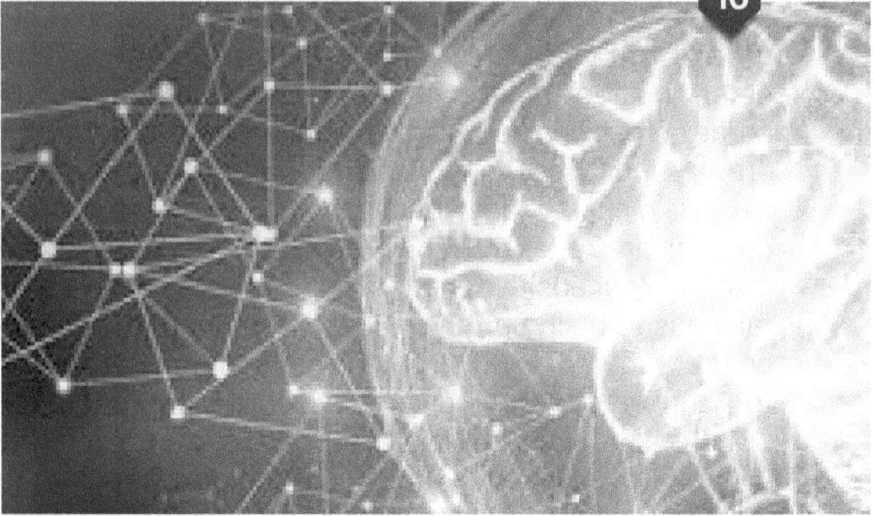

WHAT ELSE CAN YOU DO?

Chapter Ten

WHAT ELSE CAN YOU DO?

Energy Channelling

Nobody has unlimited energy level for drive, even though many over achievers look like they do. The secret of over achievers is the proper channelling of their energy. Have you been to a game as a mere spectator and ended up with bruised skin, coarse voice, and wasted muscles when leaving the sport arena? Even the participant in the game may not be as tired as you are after the game. When they were doing tens of miles on the pitch, you would have ended up doing double of that on one spot in the stand where you were watching from. While the players ended up with a day job done and accolades, you will end up with the satisfaction of a passionate fan being entertained and expressive. Both are profitable and fulfilling, but one will get the bill paid.

The caveat is that not all motions produce profit. In order to make significant profits out of your enormous energy level, you need to know how to channel the motion into what profits.

Lesson # 28 – Not every motion mean progress.

Pursuit of Profits
When energy is not properly channelled, it ends up wearing out and burning up the bearer. Think of the massive heat energy generated in nuclear reactors, which has to be channelled at turning water into steam, which generates turbine motion to ultimately create electrical energy in a power plant. If the energy was not properly channelled, the heat would become detrimental to the reactor and probably burn it up to create an explosion.

* The late Nelson Mandela of South Africa was a global icon and global elder statesman till death with an enormous positive influence on humanity even after death. It wasn't always like that. History showed us that many Western super powers neither acceded to his person nor the movement he represented till the unfolding of events after his release from the prison. The positive energy of gaining freedom was channelled into healing and reconciliation, which started when he decided to forgive all those that did him and his people wrong. The euphoria of freedom could have been wasted on debauchery or wrongly channelled into vengeance, retaliation and vindictiveness. The end justified the means for the statesman. He died a global icon of peace, wisdom, and progressiveness worthy of emulation.

Edge of Change
On many occasions, big changes occur by small happenings. When you find yourself in such an intersection of life, make the most of it.

Part of human intelligence is the capacity to channel what is generated into the edge desired. Whenever an event brings you to the edge, take the advantage of it and channel that energy into profitable curve.

There is something referred to as gaining and being in momentum in sport. It is a combination of renewed energy, hope, and drive to win that surges within a player or within a team when the opponent yields a little ground in a game that was otherwise being lost. When this happens, leeway is created for change in the game and smart athletes, and teams leverage it for a quantum leap of taking the lead. We have seen such edge wasted on many occasions.

Just as in
sport, you will be presented with very fragile game-changing edges of change in momentum with which you can create the following real curves of turnaround if well managed.

When the change in momentum comes in your life as in a game: watch out for and leverage on these, they are the positive energy at work:

1   *Hope to win is renewed.*
2   *Confidence is birthed.*
3   *Damage to self-esteem repaired.*
4   *Damage to team spirit repaired.*
5   *Blame game disappears.*
7   *Humiliation averted.*
8   *Past errors and mistakes are atoned for.*
9   *Sense of tiredness disappears.*
10   *Self-pity fades away.*
11   *Frustration lifts and error margin reduces.*
12   *Player starts believing in oneself.*

13   *Others' faith in you the player starts increasing.*

14   *Boiling anger at everything and nothing goes away.*

15   *There is a new zeal to get the job done.*

16   *Readiness to go extra mile.*

17   *Focus toward the finish line becomes sharper.*

18   *Desire to finish strong becomes strong.*

19   *Low probability becomes high possibility.*

20   *Upset can be created,*

21   *Record can be broken.*

22   *Latent champions within can be discovered.*

23   *New winning patterns can be created for others.*

24   *Winning way increased.*

25   *Much needed lesson learnt.*

Lesson # 29 – Don't play with little chance; that may be all there is to gain the edge.

In Pursuit of Growth

One of the primary attributes that distinguishes adults from children is wastage. You can imagine how much energy we were allowed by nature to burn when we were young. As far as children are concerned, life is a playground, but this perspective changes once we are grown up. Life becomes serious business where wastage can be costly. Children want to play all the time, but the adults will decline to join them, not for lack of energy but for the fact that we have better things we want to invest the energy in before we all shut down for the day. What primarily accounts for the difference between a child and an adult is growth.

-   *Growth helps you channel your energy profitably.*
-   *Growth is recorded as age.*
-   *Growth is accounted for by progress.*

Chronological Age - This is the measurement of the time you have been given from birth.

Mental Age -This is the measurement of development you have undergone in your faculties by learning and unlearning over the time.

Emotional Age – This is the measurement of the evolvement you have allowed to shape your personality expression over time.

Conserve Energy

Grown ups block leakages while children may be indifferent or see it as fun. Vital energy you need for progress and drive in the majors of life must not be allowed to leak away. As a grown-up, you need to recognise what takes away your drive and block it off as a leakage.

Around you will be many people and events that are always ready to puncture the energy balloon for you. What justifies your age is your growth. And what signifies your growth is your ability to block such off your energy balloon. You need your energy for better things and profiting.

Lesson # 30 -Every resource on earth is finite; stop wastage.

Create the Right Influence

We learn to do most of what we do because we saw someone else do, if not same, at least something similar. We stood up from all fours as children because we saw adults standing erect. We walk because we saw adult walking. The same goes for talking and much more. These basic but essential activities of life were not just left by nature for us to learn by mere instinct in order to underscore the power of influence. The energy influence we participate in creating or allow to be created around us is very important.

- *It can be of fear or of boldness.*
- *It can be of low probability or high possibility.*
- *It can be of love or hatred.*
- *It can be of inclusiveness or prejudice.*
- *It can enhance communal spirit or create isolation.*
- *It can be of optimism or pessimism.*
- *It can be to do good or wrong.*
- *It can promote peace or encourage war.*
- *It can encourage winning or glorify losing.*
- *It may promote excellence or fester mediocrity.*

The list goes on, and it can either be of positive energy influence or negative. The stake is high, and so the choice is deep. The environment created determines what can be cultivated therein.

When you show up, influence is created and destroyed in a positive or negative dimension based on the dominant energy you bring. People who create influence of positive energy are desirable to be with, work with, or live with. They are the ones who are well missed when not around. They help others go the right way and extra mile.

Let's Have Some Positive Energy Display
Positive energy has a way of showing in our countenance. No employer wants a sullen applicant with forlorn written all over the face. Nature desires timely dressing and trimming, else everywhere will be taken over by the wild. In a similar manner, countenance must be dressed and trimmed to project

positivity. There may be occasions of anger, sadness, and distress showing in your countenance, but it must not be your default expression.

Lesson # 31 - Life is painfully trying enough for many. What they need is not another deposit of bad energy.

* From general information available on the subject.

ENERGY
INFLUENCE
ON PERSONAL
AURA

Chapter Eleven

ENERGY INFLUENCE ON PERSONAL AURA

The energy at work in a person or group of people cannot be seen, but the drive and effects the energy creates will ultimately be visible. The aura created can easily tell us whether we are dealing with the positive or negative shade of energy. On a lighter mood over the next four chapters, we shall be examining the possible common influence of aura created by positive and negative energy around a person, within teams, around leaders and in relationships.

For maximum impact, I will be using bullet points and sub-points to highlight the discussion. The starting point is the influence both positive and negative energy exact on the personal aura and how they influence the character, behaviour and personality of an individual.

1.   Demeanour and Deportment
- Positive energy brings more elations and happiness when at work in abundance; while negative energy builds up more frustration and precipitate depression.
- Positive energy brings goodwill and opens doors of opportunities to the driven; whereas resentments and shut doors easily come the way of negativity.

- Positive energy enhances good self-esteem and builds confidence around you; while negative energy destroys self-esteem, nose dives confidence, helps play the victim and employs emotional blackmail for expression.

2.   **On Productivity**
- Positive energy gravitates towards the needed platforms of expression for innate abilities; whereas negative energy repels enabling platforms.
- Positive energy enhances personal productivity by opening up the mind to beneficial ideas. Negative energy shuts down personal productivity centre as it closes up the mind to any beneficial idea.
- Positive energy helps to persist and persevere for the result, but negative energy helps to easily get frustrated and give up.
- Positive energy makes the driven become desirable employee and productive subordinates. Negative energy helps to create a not so desirable employee and poor subordinate.

3.   **In Trouble and Challenges**
- With positive energy, people surmount difficult task, simplify complications and make hard challenges seem easy. Whereas, negative energy makes a mountain of every task, even when such task is simple.
- Positive energy strives to brings goods out of the dry and poisoned environment, but negative energy poisons good environments and makes them dry and toxic.
- Positive energy helps the troubled shake off the dust with focus on getting up, coming out and moving on. They cannot be held hostage by challenges of life. Negative energy imprisons the mind and holds the victim hostage in the gulag of trouble.

- Positive energy motivates the driven to keep seeking a solution to the challenges at hand, even if the solution seems so far away or won't be found. Negative energy makes the driven to sub-consciously avoid solutions even if it glaringly stares everyone in the face.

4.　　In Failure and Disappointment

- Positive energy helps to take responsibility, even when it can be easily shifted. Whereas, negative energy plays blame game, even when it is inconsequential.

- With positive energy, people make an effort to wipe off bad memories, let go of the bad past and refuse to be a prisoner of personal mistakes. Negative energy attached people to the bad past like glue and brings it up at every slight opportunity and revel in building infinite storage capacity for evil recollection.

- Happy times are more than moody times in the face of challenges when the energy is positive; but moody, damp and sullen is the default of negativity.

- Positive energy is not an amplifier of mistakes of others, but negative energy cannot let the mistakes of others pass through any narrow gate.

- Positive energy helps the driven to give life another shot again and again after failure, but negative energy cannot look or move past personal mistakes.

5.　　On Gifts Rights and Privileges

- Positive energy sees endowments as an opportunity to do good for mankind; whereas negative energy sees endowments as the exclusivity of being superhuman.

- Positive energy uses gifts and talents as a rare privilege to maximize positive impact, but negative energy uses gifts and talents for mere aggrandizement.

- One driven by positive energy has a good sense of gratitude, but negative energy gives a serious sense of entitlement.

6. On Life Outlook and Paradigm
- Positive energy makes people enjoy life and focus on living happily. Whereas, negative energy makes people resent life, always angry and complaining about something.
- Positive energy makes people look bright and feel healthy even in the face of health challenges. Negative energy makes people to always look tired, weak and feels moribund even when nothing is wrong.
- Positive energy rejoices when good things happen to others or in the world. Negative energy is indifferent to good news and can even be sadistic.
- Positive energy makes more friends even among enemies, but negative energy makes more enemies even among friends and relations.
- One driven of positive energy are the binding agents among friends and relations; whereas the scattering agent amongst friend and relations are always driven by negativity.
- Positive energy lights up the party but negative energy dampens the moods and fouls up the party.
- The one dominated by positive energy focuses on cause and effects, but one driven by negative energy focuses on luck, is fixated on conspiracies and engulfed with mysteries.

7. When Someone needs to be Around
- People with positive energy are good to have around when you are down, as they will lift you the right way and

in the right direction; whereas the ones driven by negative energy will make you feel worse in your down moments.

- Positive energy driven people are good to have around when celebrating, they help your joy; but the ones driven by negative energy may dampen up the atmosphere suddenly with mood swing, even on trivialities.

8.   **On Religion Faith and Believe System**
- Positive energy uses religion and faith as personal choices of affirmations for personal development and self-evolvement. Negative energy uses faith and religion as an excuse for retardation and self-destruction.
- Uses faith and religion to benefit others, community, and humanity at large; negative energy uses faith and religion as an excuse for hatred of others and the destruction of mankind.

9.   **With Race Tribe and Nationality**
- Positive energy uses human differences such as nationalities, tribes and races to appreciate diversities in humanity; whereas, negative energy uses nationality, tribe and race to promote hatred and bigotry.
- Positive energy uses human differences such as nationality, tribe, and race to promote fairness, equity, and justice. Negative energy uses human differences such as nationality, tribe, and race for injustice and discrimination.
- Positive energy uses human differences such as nationality, tribe and race to the benefit and profiting of all. Negative energy uses human differences such as nationality, tribe and race for extortion.

## 10.	When in Anger and Low Emotional State

- Positive energy is rational in anger and weighs consequences of actions to be taken; whereas negative energy is irrational with no regard for consequences when angry.

- Positive energy measures words and actions in anger to forestall damages to relationships, but negative energy uses expletives without caution to destroy relationships when in anger.

- Positive energy avoids harm to people and destructions of goods when angry; negative energy is bent on creating harm and found of destructions of properties when in anger.

- With positive energy, happy and feel good times dominate the rare and extremely occasional times of sadness and mood. With negative energy, moody times dominates the very rare and occasional happy times.

## 11.	When in Competition

- Positive energy takes up healthy competitions as a good challenge when it is inevitable and uses the challenge to push for personal excellence. Negative energy makes healthy competition become unhealthy and a personality war.

- One driven by positive energy is not given to unnecessary and inconsequential petty competition that bothers on mere rivalry. Negative energy has an unhealthy appetite for rivalry, even in things that aren't competitive.

- Positive energy makes competitive activities such as sport fun even when challenging for mastery; whereas, negative energy makes the same competitive activities created for fun to become very toxic.

12. In Builder

- Positive energy makes people channel their efforts into building good things of life such as home, organization, relationship, venture, reputation and many more. The ones that are driven by negative energy use the better part of their efforts to specialize in mocking, analyse, antagonize, criticize and pull down those that are building something.

- One driven by positive energy avoid pulling down the house when in conflicts; but tries to preserve order and investments. Negativity doesn't mind if the house come crashing down on everyone and every investment is wasted.

- Positive energy makes you feel it's possible to build, whereas the negative energy scares you off your possibilities of building something worthwhile.

13. On Work and Project

- Positive energy is enthusiastic about work and focussed on the goal. Negative energy is lethargic about work easily distracted from the goal.

- Positive energy builds up projection with wise plans ahead, but negative energy is obsessed with the immediate and now, with little regard for tomorrow.

- Positive energy makes you proactive and full of initiatives on tasks; whereas negative energy is only reactive to the problem and lacking in initiatives on task.

- Positive energy sees projects to desirable end and logical conclusions; while negative energy path is filled with inconclusive works and littered with abandoned projects.

- Positive energy makes a way in the rock, but negative energy meets with a brick wall at every turn of the event.

14. Relaxation and Recreation

- Positivity is not lacking in fun but measured in pastime and relaxation; whereas negative energy makes people major in fun seeking and expend all time and productive energy on pastime and relaxation.
- Positive energy rejoices in success and enjoys the good fruits of labour, but negative energy uses false humility to avoid embracing success and guilt to demonise enjoying the good fruits of labour.

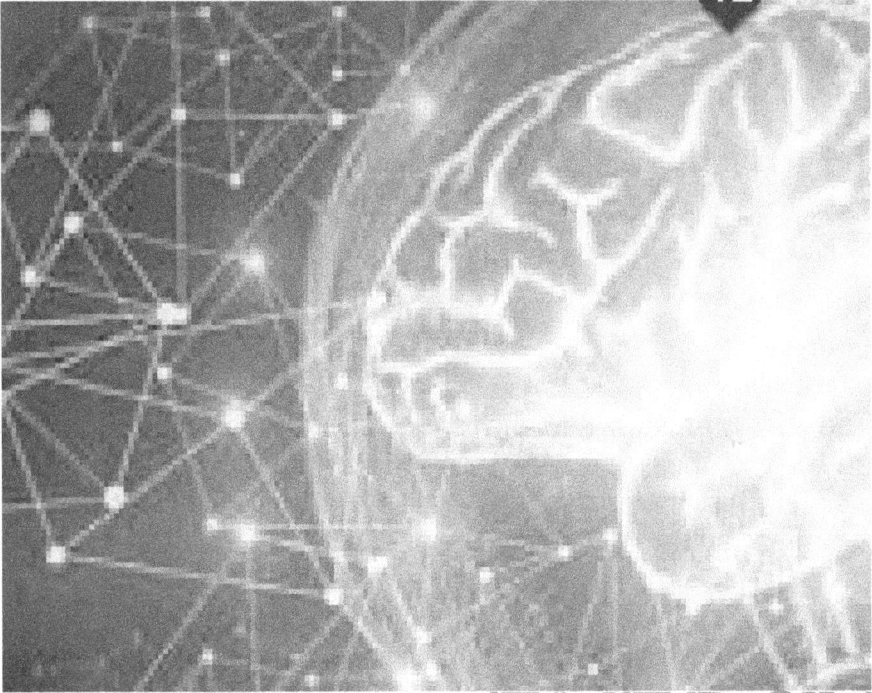

ENERGY
INFLUENCE
ON TEAM
AURA

ENERGY INFLUENCE ON TEAM AURA

The energy at work in a team cannot be visualized, but the drive and effects the energy creates within the team will ultimately be visible. This accounts for the team's progress, cohesion and seamless delivery of the team mandate or otherwise.

The aura of influence created within a team can easily tell us whether we are dealing with a dominant positive or negative shade of energy in the team. We can narrow it down to the members as individual by truthful insight into what is brought to the table by individual and what is allowed on the table by the team.

1. **Being a Part of the Entity**
   - Positive energy driven are good team players in the task so required. Negative energy driven is solo, selfish and individualistic in what requires a team effort.
   - Positive energy driven are committed to bringing what is required of them to the table; whereas, negative energy focuses on what others must bring to the table.
   - Positive energy recognizes what others bring to the table with a good attitude even when there is the need for improvement, but negative energy is so fixated on their

own contributions that they can't see what others are doing to help the team.

- Positive energy helps the driven to be loyal to team goals and objectives all the way, but negative energy pushes people to betray team goals and objectives at a slight push.
- Team members with dominant positive energy are loyal to other team members and seek their success in the team task, but the ones dominated by negative energy are not loyal to anyone but themself.
- Positive energy loves unity and harmony in the group. Ones driven by negative energy crave quarrel, chaos and divisive caucuses.
- Positive energy strives to be a binding agent in the team; while negative energy is readily available as a scattering agent and sow seeds of discord.
- Team members driven by positive energy know that they owe the team the needed performance and responsibility. Whereas, negative energy confers an undue sense of entitlement.
- Team members dealing in positive energy feel at home in a high-performance environment. Team members struggling with negative energy always feel lost and persecuted in a high-performance environment.
- People driven by positive energy have the utmost respect for the laid down rules and regulations as long as they are within the team. Negative energy makes people have little or no regard for team rules and regulations.
- Team members driven by positive energy recognise team authority and leadership with respect for team hierarchal structure. Team members driven by negative energy undermine leadership, disdain authority and have little or no respect for hierarchy.

2. Personal Ambition and Team Goal Equilibrium

- Team goal supersedes personal ambition for positive energy, negative energy puts personal glory ahead of the team success.
- Positive energy seeks success and personal fulfilment in tandem to team success, whereas negative energy seeks personal excellence even if at the expense of the team success.
- Positive energy helps people to still be happy if others in the team happen to get the most attention; but negative energy makes them become petty, seeking attention at all costs.
- Positive energy brings what will help the team to succeed even if it won't get the glory. Negative energy drives people to conceal what could help the team succeed as long as they won't get the glory personally.

3. Criticism Within Team

- Positive energy brings constructive criticism aimed at helping recipients improve without feeling worthless altogether. Negative energy fuels destructive critic aimed at pulling the recipient down as one who has nothing good whatsoever to offer in the team.
- Positive energy loves showing a good way by example rather than mere criticism. Negative energy is all talks and less actions to show the right way by example.
- Positive energy uses mild style and tact to pass across criticism; whereas negative energy is brash and caustic in criticism.
- Positive energy uses a private session with the team member to offer criticism and minimize embarrassment; negative energy prefers open criticism even when the private option is available.

- Positive energy helps people to take criticism within the team on board with a good attitude when they are on the receiving end. People driven by negative energy have the attitude of being persecuted and picked on, even when the concern raised is genuine.
- Positive energy helps the recipient of criticism to pick up soon and move on with the task ahead with an undiminished drive. Negative energy beclouds the mind of people with discouragement and takes their drive away once they are criticised, even when it is needful.

4. When Team Succeeds
- Positive energy easily shares the glory as an outcome of team efforts. Negative energy sits upon and personalizes the glory of team efforts.
- Positive energy is still happy with the team success even when not singled out for praise by authority; negative energy wants to be personally recognised by all means.
- The ones driven by positive energy do not mind if others get a larger share of praise in team success as long as the team succeeds. Negative energy wants the largest share of praise no matter how minimal they contribute.
- One driven by positive energy seeks personal improvement to contribute more to the team's future success. Negative energy makes people to only seek immediate reward and nothing beyond.
- Positive energy makes members seek team improvement at all costs even when doing well and succeeding, but negative energy sees improvement as an unnecessary burden that demands too much personal and team adjustment.

5. When the Team Fails

- Positive energy driven one sees him/herself as part of the team failure even when he or she is not directly responsible for the failure; Negative energy passes the buck of responsibility at slight sign of failure.
- Positive energy is not pointing the finger and saying I said so as if it's been waiting all along for the team to fail. Negative energy is full of retrospective exoneration of self from the cause and effect.
- Positive energy is determined to lift the team out of the pit as much as it can, but negative energy is there as observant and commentator with minimal helping hand in lifting the team.
- Positive energy helps other team members to also do their best for the team to turn the curve. One driven by negative energy, out of a craving for self-glory, prefers to look like the only one doing the needful.

6. When Leaving

- Team members driven by positive energy leave the team voluntarily if continuous stay is detrimental and counterproductive to the team; one driven by negative energy will rather be pushed even when staying is obviously counterproductive.
- Positive energy will rather leave than being toxic and lethargic and divisive within the team; negative energy stays to spill toxicity, create lethargy and divide the team.
- Those driven by positive energy exits the team with minimal loss or damages to the team if leaving is inevitable. People driven by negative energy tries hard for the team to collapse upon their exit.
- Team members driven by positive energy leave great and awesome memories behind upon leaving. Whereas the

ones driven by negative energy leave wounds and tears behind upon exit.

7. When There is Conflict
- Positive energy seeks an amicable resolution to conflicts within the team, but negative energy will rather escalate crisis into a conflagration.
- Positive energy helps the team member to follow and submit to the laid down procedure for conflict resolution. Negative energy prefers to shift the post in the midst of a match for undue personal advantage.
- The one driven with positive energy will fight solo without smearing others if fighting is inevitable. Negative energy makes the fighter drag as many into the conflict in order to create anarchy.
- If there is conflict, positive energy will still respect mutual confidence shared in the past, except when non-sharing borders on criminality. Negative energy crosses all lines and breaks all rules of mutual confidence once there is conflict, just to get even or extract maximum damage.

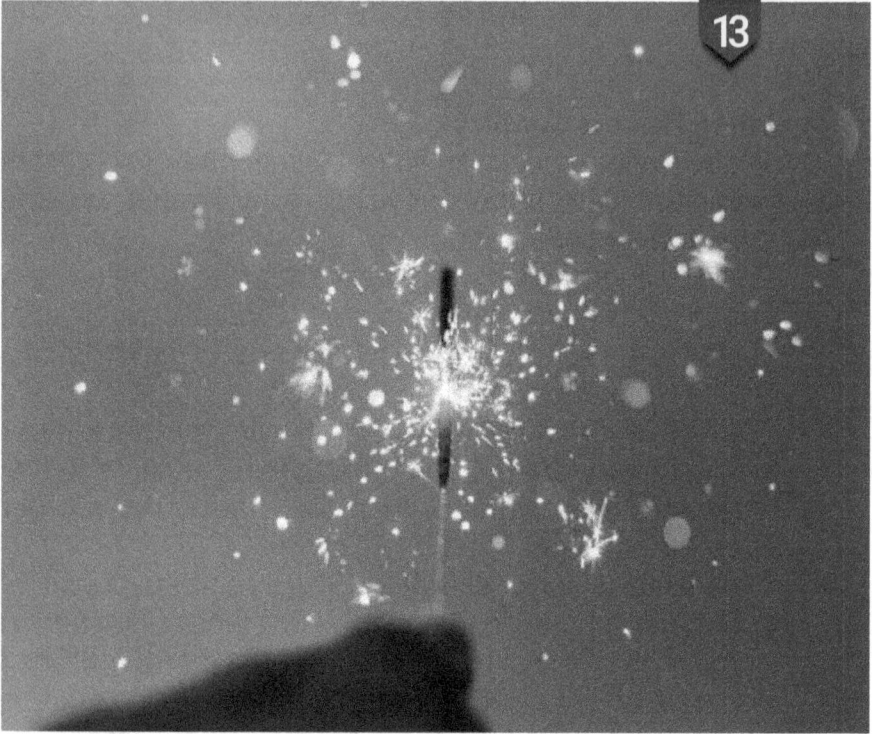

ENERGY INFLUENCE ON LEADERSHIP AURA

ENERGY INFLUENCE ON LEADERSHIP AURA

The energy at work in a leader cannot be visualised, but the drive and effects the energy creates in the leadership will ultimately be visible. This accounts for peaceful, progressive, innovative, well loved, well accepted and prosperous leadership or otherwise.

The aura of influence created around a leader can easily tell us whether we are dealing with a leader with a dominant positive or negative shade of energy. We can narrow it down to personality traits and what is brought to the table as leadership skills.

1.   Here Comes the Boss
- Leaders that are driven by positive energy see leadership as a rare privilege; whereas, leaders driven by negative energy see leadership as a bestowment of right and an entitlement of merit.
- Leaders that are driven by positive energy see leadership as a platform to serve others, but the one driven by negative energy see leadership as the ultimate opportunity to be served.
- Positive energy driven ones are good employers; whereas, negative energy driven ones are bad employers.

- Leaders driven by positive energy are supportive bosses; while the ones driven by negative energy are discouraging bosses.
- Leaders driven by positive energy are seen as great boss by subordinates; whereas, the ones driven by negative energy are seen as a horrible boss.
- Leaders driven by positive energy are not predators on subordinates; Leaders driven by negative energy use power to exploit the subordinates.
- Positive energy driven leaders are approachable while maintaining the office decorum and hierarchal sanctity. Negative energy driven leaders are full of airs and graces which make approach almost impossible.
- Leaders driven by positive energy are happy and lively; they also want others to be happy and lively as they are. Leaders driven by negative energy are cantankerous and want others to be miserable too.

2.   **When in Power**
- Leaders driven by positive energy are kind and empathetic, but leaders driven by negative energy are cruel and callous.
- Positive energy driven leaders tend to use power to alleviate the subordinate, but the ones that are driven by negative energy use power to suppress and oppress followers and subordinates.
- Leaders that are driven by positive energy use power to promote good course for the benefit of many. Leaders driven by negative energy are self-serving with minimal goodwill to others.

- Positive energy controls the corrupting tendency of power. Negative energy corrupts power.
- Leaders driven by positive energy are confident and secure; negative energy breeds insecurity in leaders.
- Positive energy makes leaders less controlling, but negative energy pushes leaders to use power for maximal and excessive control of others.

3.   **Subordinates and Followers**
- Leaders driven by positive energy are supportive of their subordinate in accordance with and even beyond the letter. Leaders that are driven by negative energy see subordinate as a tool to just be used and cleaned and not supported beyond that.
- Positive energy driven leader allows for the development of those beneath them into higher places and leadership; whereas leaders driven by negative energy have no room for the emergence of the subordinate.
- Positive energy leader boosts the confidence of the subordinates. Negative energy driven leader takes away and destroys the confidence of the subordinates.
- Leader driven by positive energy helps subordinates build a positive image and visible profile. Leaders driven by negative energy revels at the humiliation of subordinates and prefers them hidden.
- Leaders driven by positive energy support the evolvement of subordinates into a bigger star; Leaders driven by negative energy cannot stand another rising star, talk less of a bigger one.

4. Leader During Crisis

- Leaders driven by positive energy have it at the back of their mind that they have institutions and structures to protect from damage. Leaders that are driven by negative energy expose institutions and structures to all possible damage brought by a crisis.

- Leaders driven by positive energy are proactive and have crisis resolution structures in place ahead of the crisis. Leaders driven by negative energy do not envisage nor plan ahead of the crisis.

- Leaders driven by positive energy protect subordinates, especially the vulnerable one, in time of crisis. Leaders driven by negative energy first and foremost seek to save their own nest and head at the expense of the team.

- Leaders driven by positive energy seek genuine cause and effect of the crisis in order to address them; leaders driven by negative energy are looking for who to blame and exoneration of self.

5. Boss in Conflict

- Leaders that are driven by positive energy handle conflict as stakeholders; leaders driven by negative energy handle conflict as if nothing is at stake.

- Leaders that are driven by positive energy seeks peace at all cost. Leaders that are driven by negative energy drum for war at a slight push.

- Leaders that are driven by positive energy consider the cost of conflict before stepping into it; the ones driven by negative energy are blinded to cost of war.

- Leaders that are driven by positive energy regrets their avoidable involvement and undesirable effect of conflict. Leaders driven by negative energy have no afterthought of regret even when the unavoidable damages of conflicts surround them.

6.   Glory and Responsibility
- Leaders driven by positive energy easily shares the glory with subordinates, especially the ones with crucial contributions. Leaders that are driven by negative energy corner and keep the glory to themselves even if the vital task was wholly undertaken by subordinates.
- Leaders that are driven by positive energy take the responsibility all the way; the ones which are driven by negative energy hate and shift the responsibility somewhere else.

7.   Rewards and Retributions
- Leaders driven with positive energy believe in and bestow the fitting financial reward deem appropriate for the service rendered by the subordinate. Whereas, leaders driven by negative energy do not believe in and do withhold financial reward deem appropriate for the service rendered by the subordinate.
- Leaders driven by positive energy bestow appropriate goodwill such as promotion and other non-financial rewards deem appropriate for the service rendered by the subordinate. Leaders who are driven by negative energy withhold goodwill such as promotion and other non-financial reward deem appropriate for the service rendered by the subordinate.
- Leaders that are driven by positive energy exact proportional punishment when inevitable; whereas, leaders who are driven by negative energy will kill a fly with a sledgehammer so to say.

- Leaders driven by positive energy are interested in correction and redemption of offenders; the ones driven by negative energy have no room for reconstruction.

8.   **When Exit is the Way**
- Leaders that are driven by positive energy leave when the ovations are loud; the one driven by negative energy insist on dancing when the music has stopped.
- Leaders who are driven by positive energy choose to leave if presence becomes toxic and burdensome to the institution, but the one driven with negative energy will stay to spill the toxicity and cripple the institution form going forward.
- Leaders that are driven with positive energy leave with no or minimal but inevitable damage to the institution; leaders driven with negative energy leave with so much crisis and chaos left behind.
- Leaders that are driven by positive energy focus on building and leaving better and sustainable structure behind upon exit. Leaders that are driven by negative energy weaken or erode existing organisational structure and leaving non-sustainable ones behind upon exit.
- Leaders driven by positive energy follow the laid down rule of leaving great successor in place upon exit. Leaders that are driven with negative energy bastardise the system to create good leadership vacuum and or total leadership crisis upon exit.

ENERGY
INFLUENCE ON
RELATIONSHIP
AURA

ENERGY INFLUENCE ON RELATIONSHIP AURA

Relationship in this context ranges from friendship to partnership in its various capacities. The energy at work in any relationship cannot be visualised as well, but the drive and effects the energy creates in the relationship will ultimately be visible. This accounts for cordiality, friendship, love, synergy, progress, happiness and fulfilment experienced in the relationship or otherwise.

The aura of influence created within any relationship can easily tell us whether we are dealing with a good relationship with dominant positive energy or a toxic relationship with the dominant negative shade of energy. We can as well narrow it down to the personalities involved and what is brought to the table by individual involved.

1. **When in Relationship**
    - Positive energy enters into the relationship to give and receive love; whereas, negative energy enters a relationship to use or torment partner with needy mindset. Such ones are too engrossed in self and need for love that they cannot look after anyone else or give love.

- Positive energy driven partners brighten up the day and enhance the lives around them. The ones who are driven with negative energy mess up people's day and lives ultimately.

- Positive energy driven people strive to enhance friendship and show love; But negative energy breeds bitterness, creates resentment and fosters hatred.

- People driven by positive energy make good things happen for others. The ones driven by negative energy do much to foul up others' aura.

- People with an abundance of positive energy rub it off on their partners thereby helping them to be more positive than before. The ones with much of negative energy bring an enormous deposit of negativity into relationships thereby making their partner imbibe more negativity than ever before.

- Positive energy driven ones make partners look and feel that they are better than they actually are; negative energy is condescending and put the other party down at slight provocation in order to feel bigger and better.

- People driven with positive energy boost others self-esteem; whereas the ones that are driven with negative energy use the art of putting others down to gain control and feel important.

- People driven by positive energy are empathetic and compassionate but the ones driven by negative energy are callous and merciless.

- People who are driven by positive energy stand up for the less privileged and fight their cause for justice and fairness. The ones driven by negative energy takes advantage of the less privileged and use their cause for aggrandizement.

2.   When in Conflict

- The one driven by positive energy looks inward first, but the negative energy driven ones point finger first
- One driven by positive energy seeks self-improvement first, but the one driven with negative energy sees no need to improve. For such, it is the other party that is always at fault and need to improve.
- The one driven by positive energy seeks to help the other party to improve, but the one driven by negative energy is demanding improvement without helping hand.
- Positive energy argues and maintains cordiality to keep relationships. Negative energy argues with expletives to ruin relationships.
- Positive energy is mindful of potential damage words and action can cause, but negative energy cares less about whose ox is gored.

3.   Dealing with the Human Web

- People driven with positive energy have the utmost regard for human relationships and do their best to keep them cordial. The ones driven by negative energy have little regard for human relationship and can ruin any relationship at will.
- People driven by positive energy have regards for and do their best to be value adding part of the community. People driven by negative energy are always disconnected from community and dangerous to humanity.
- People driven by positive energy have regard for associations, but the ones driven by negative energy are always bigger and better than any association in their own eyes.
- People driven by positive energy have respect for

human web and connectivity, but the ones driven by negative energy are Isolated and exclusionists.

4.   **When Leaving**
   - People driven by positive energy leave partners in a better position than they met them if they have to leave; but the one driven by negative energy leave messed up partners behind.
   - The one driven by positive energy cares more about the feeling of others and so make leaving less traumatic. The ones that are driven by negative energy always want leaving to be as traumatic as possible to validate the basal feeling of self-importance.
   - Positive energy driven ones take time to look after the interest of the other party in the parting arrangement. Whereas, the ones driven by negative energy is only interested in personal gain upon leaving.

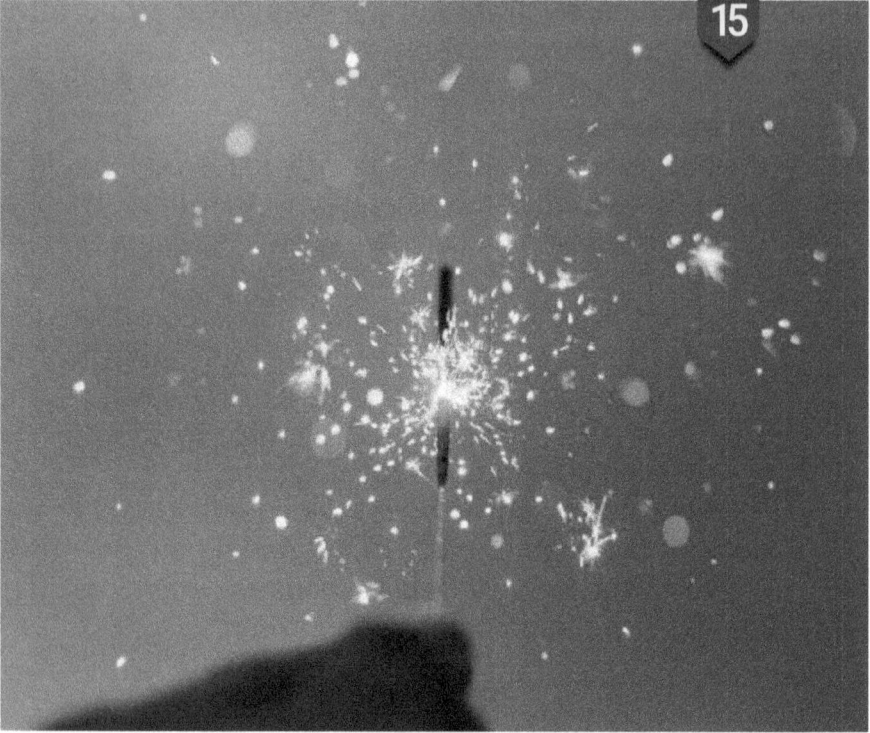

ENERGY
INDICES

Chapter Fifteen

ENERGY INDICES

Not Standardised

Let's just have a quick exercise that you can apply in your energy self-assessment and create improvement or radical change, depending on what you require. It is not a standardised assessment, neither is it a holy grail for everyone. You can grade your energy charge and level on a calibrated scale.

If you are mathematically savvy, you can create a constant and derive your own energy index formula if it helps you. For the purpose of this publication, we will create a simple linear scale of horizontal dimensions depicting dominant charge and the degree of dominance.

Note that the energy markers for personality traits are somewhat inclusive and being added to every other area we want to assess. This is simply because the formatting pedestal is first in the personality of whoever is being assessed.

The test and result is valid for the time you took it. Just as disposition and response are subject to change per time so the result and the need to do more assessment over the time.

Quantum Index

Being positively or negatively charged per moment is as clear as noonday, but to be sufficiently charged aright is the target. This is the reflection of the degree of negativity or positivity per given time or per given area you are assessing. You can apply this to a particular issue or your energy charge in general. Your aim is to always migrate rightward per time. The migration can be unending as you desire.

- Check the dominant marker by comparing how many is ticked in either section. A simple majority indicates dominant positive or negative energy in the test.
- If the energy charge is positive, calculate the ratio of the positive marker you tick to the total positive marker you were assessed on. Simply put, divide your positive marker score by the total positive marker.
- If the energy charge is negative, calculate the ratio of the negative marker you tick to the total marker you were assessed on. Simply put, divide your negative score by the total negative marker.
- Any fraction below $1/3 = 1$.
- Any fraction between $1/3$ and $2/3 = 2$.
- Any fraction above $2/3 = 3$.
- The charge can then be applied as applicable.

The interpretation can then be deduced as:
+1 = Just Positive
+2 = Very Positive
+3 = Extremely Positive
-1 = Just Negative
-2 = Very Negative
-3 = Extremely Negative

1.   Energy Indices for Personality Trait

- You can create a simple energy index by drawing a horizontal line with -3 and the extreme left and +3 at the extreme right of the line.
- Fill up the numbers in between these extremes, with 0 at the centre. This line represents the energy charge chart. (optional).
- Check yourself against the markers below.
- Where you tick the higher number signifies your dominant energy charge
  for the moment, whether it is positive or negative.
- You can indicate this on your line if you chose the line option; positive (right) and negative (left).

POSITIVE ENERGY MARKERS FOR PERSONALITY TRAITS

1	Brings you more elation and happiness.
2	Brings goodwill to you.
3	Opens doors of opportunities.
4	Brings platforms of expression for innate abilities.
5	Brings goods out of dry or poisoned environment.
6	Enhances good self-esteem and builds confidence.
7	Rejoices when good things happen to others or in the world.
8	Shakes off the dust and cannot be held hostage by challenges of life.

9	Takes responsibility, even when it can be easily shifted.
10	Seeks solution always, even if it won't be found.
11	Happy times are more than moody times.
12	Makes effort to detach from and let go of a bad past.
13	Makes efforts to wipe out bad memories.
14	Not a prisoner of personal mistakes.
15	Not an amplifier of mistakes of others.
16	Desirable employee and productive subordinate.
17	Uses gifts, talents, and endowments for general good of mankind.
18	Good sense of gratitude.
19	Enjoys life and living happily.
20	Looks strong and feels healthy even in the face of a health challenge.
21	Makes more friends even among enemies.
22	Binding agent among friends and relations.
23	Lights up the party.
24	Good to have around when you are down.
25	Good to have around when celebrating.
26	Makes competitive activities such as sports fun even when challenging for mastery.
27	Uses personal choices of affirmations such as faith and religion for personal evolvement.
28	Uses personal choices of affirmations such as faith and religion to benefit others.

29	Uses human differences such as nationalities, tribes, and races to appreciate diversities in humanity.
30	Rationalise and weighs consequences.
31	Measures words and actions in anger to forestall damage and destruction.
32	Focuses on cause and effect.

NEGATIVE ENERGY MARKERS IN PERSONALITY TRAITS

1	Builds up more frustration and depression within.
2	Generates repulsion from and towards others.
3	Shuts doors of opportunities against the pursuit.
4	Meets with brick wall at every turn in pursuits.
5	Poisons good environments and makes them dry and toxic for pursuits.
6	Destroys good self-esteem and nose dives confidence.
7	Indifferent to good news and even can be sadistic.
8	Plays the victim and employs emotional blackmail for expression.
9	Plays blame game, even when it is inconsequential.
10	Avoids solution even if it glaringly stares everyone in the face.
11	Moody times dominates the very rare and occasional happy times.
12	Attached to the bad past and brings up at the slight opportunity.
13	Revels in building infinite storage capacity for recollection of bad.
14	Cannot look or move past personal mistakes in past or present pursuit.
15	Cannot let the mistakes of others pass through any narrow gate.
16	Not-so-desirable employee and poor subordinate.
17	Sees gifts, talents, and endowments as exclusive rights and not privileges.

18	Serious sense of entitlement.
19	Resents life and always angry about something.
20	Looks weak and feels moribund even when nothing is wrong.
21	Makes more enemies even among friends against the pursuit.
22	Scattering agent amongst friend and relations.
23	Sullen and fouls up the party.
24	Will make you feel worse in your down moments.
25	May dampen the atmosphere suddenly.
26	Makes competitive activities such as sports very toxic.
27	Uses faith and religion as excuse for failure in pursuits.
28	Uses faith and religion as excuse to breed hatred for others in good pursuits.
29	Uses nationality, tribes, and races to promote hatred, exploitation, and bigotry.
30	Irrational with no regard for consequences.
31	Uses words and actions in angers to cause irreparable damage and destruction to the pursuit.
32	Focuses on luck, conspiracies, and mysteries when in pursuit

- Calculate the ratio of the positive marker you tick to the total positive marker you were assessed on. Simply put, divide your positive marker score by 32. It indicates the degree of your positivity in pursuit.
- Calculate the ratio of the negative marker you tick to the total marker you were assessed on. Simply put, divide your negative score by 32. It indicates the degree of your negativity in pursuit.
- Any fraction below 1/3 = 1.
- Any fraction between 1/3 and 2/3 = 2.
- Any fraction above 2/3 = 3.
- The charge can then be applied as applicable.

The interpretation can then be deduced as:
+1 = Just Positive
+2 = Very Positive
+3 = Extremely Positive
-1 = Just Negative
-2 = Very Negative
-3 = Extremely Negative

Note – You can see how far left or right you are on the energy chart if you choose the line option.

2. Energy Indices in Personal Pursuits

- Check yourself against the markers below.
- Where you tick the higher number of energy markers signifies your dominant energy charge for the moment, whether it is positive (right) or negative (left).

POSITIVE ENERGY MARKERS FOR PERSONAL PURSUITS

1	Brings more elation and happiness to the pursuit.
2	Brings goodwill to the pursuit.
3	Opens doors of opportunities.
4	Brings platforms of expression for innate abilities.
5	Brings goods out of dry or poisoned environment of achievement.
6	Enhances good self-esteem and builds confidence for result.
7	Rejoices when good things happen to others in their good pursuit.
8	Shakes off the dust and cannot be held hostage by challenges in pursuit.
9	Takes responsibility for outcome in pursuits, even when it can be easily shifted.
10	Always seek solution on projects, even if it won't be found.
11	Happy times are more than moody times in pursuits.
12	Makes effort to detach from and let go of a bad past.
13	Makes efforts to wipe out bad memories of past failures.

14	Not a prisoner of personal mistakes while in pursuit.
15	Not an amplifier of mistakes of others associated with the pursuit.
16	Desirable partner in pursuits and projects.
17	Uses gifts, talents, and endowments as means to achieve great feat.
18	Good sense of gratitude all the way.
19	Enjoys life and living happily in spite of pursuits pressure.
20	Looks strong and good to go on assignment.
21	Makes more friends on projects.
22	Binding agent that brings all factors and of productivity together to achieve good success.
23	Lights up the field.
24	Good to have around when you are down in your own pursuits.
25	Good to have around when celebrating success in your own pursuit.
26	Makes competitive activities such as market rivalry fun even when challenging for mastery.
27	Uses personal choices of affirmations such as faith and religion for career and pursuits evolvement.
28	Uses personal choices of affirmations such as faith and religion to benefit good cause and bring drive for success.
29	Uses human differences such as nationalities, tribes, and races to appreciate how diversities in humanity can bring more success.

30	Rationalises and weighs consequences in the light of the project at hand.
31	Measures words and actions in anger to forestall irreparable damage and destruction to the pursuit.
32	Focuses on cause and effects in pursuit.
33	Always seeking enhancement of personal productivity.
34	Opens up the mind to beneficial ideas.
35	Persists and perseveres for result in pursuits.
36	Surmounts mountain in difficult task.
37	Rejoices at and enjoys the good fruits of success.
38	Takes up competition on board as good challenge and pushes for personal excellence.
39	Builder of good things – homes, organisations, relationship, ventures, reputation, and so on.
40	Avoids pulling down the house when in conflict to preserve order and investments.
41	Makes others feel it's possible to achieve.
42	Sees projects to logical end and rational conclusions.
43	Enthusiastic about work and focused on goal.
44	Not lacking but measured in pastime and relaxations.
45	Proactive and full of initiatives on tasks.
46	Positive projection with wise plans ahead.

NEGATIVE ENERGY MARKERS FOR PERSONAL PURSUITS

1	Builds up more frustration and depression within against pursuits.
2	Generates repulsion from and towards others in great pursuits.
3	Shuts doors of opportunities against the outstanding pursuit.
4	Meets with brick wall from the inside at every turn in pursuits.
5	Poisons good environments and makes them dry and toxic for progress.
6	Destroys good self-esteem and nose dives confidence needed for achievement.
7	Indifferent to good news about success and even can be sadistic towards greatness.
8	Plays the victim and employs emotional blackmail for expression of personal failure.
9	Plays blame game, even when it is inconsequential.
10	Avoids evolvement even if it glaringly stares everyone in the face.
11	Moody times dominates the very rare and occasional happy times on assignment.
12	Attached to the past failures and brings them up at the slight opportunity.
13	Revels in building infinite storage capacity for recollection of missed and messed opportunities.
14	Cannot look or move past the damage caused by past or present pursuit.

15	Cannot let the mistakes of others involved in the project pass through any narrow gate.
16	Not-so-desirable partner in pursuit of project.
17	Sees gifts, talents, and endowments as ends in themselves.
18	Serious sense of entitlement with little regard for efforts and commitment.
19	Resents needful assignments and always angry about something in the project.
20	Lazy, unmotivated and always look faintly on assignment.
21	Makes more enemies on any given assignment.
22	Jettisons initiative to bring production factor together to achieve success.
23	Sullen and fouls up the field.
24	Will make you feel worse in your down moments of your pursuit.
25	May dampen the success celebratory atmosphere suddenly.
26	Makes competitive activities such as market rivalry toxic.
27	Uses faith and religion as excuse for failure in pursuits.
28	Uses faith and religion as excuse to breed hatred for others who have good success.
29	Discountenances the use of human differences such as nationalities, tribes, and races to appreciate how diversities in humanity can bring more success.

30	Irrational with no regard for consequences in the light of project at hand.
31	Uses words and actions in angers to cause irreparable damage and destruction to the pursuit.
32	Focuses on luck, conspiracies, and mysteries when in pursuit.
33	Shuts down personal productivity centre.
34	Closes up the mind to beneficial ideas.
35	Gives up easily and full of bottled up frustration.
36	Makes a mountain of every task, even the simplest becomes so difficult.
37	Breeds false humility and uses guilt to avoid embracing success.
38	Unhealthy sense of competition to cover up for failure, even in things that aren't competitive.
39	More interested in personal-aggrandisement than legacy.
40	Doesn't mind if the house comes down crashing on everyone and every investment is wasted.
41	Scares you off your own possibilities.
42	Path filled with abandoned projects.
43	Lethargic about work; always tired, easily distracted from goal and hate lofty dreams.
44	Majors in and spends all time in idle pastime and unending relaxation.
45	Only reactive to problem and lacking in initiatives on task.
46	Obsessed with the immediate and now with little regard for tomorrow.

- Check the dominant marker by comparing how many is ticked in either section. A simple majority indicates dominant positive or negative energy in the test.
- Calculate the ratio of the positive marker you tick to the total positive marker you were assessed on. Simply put, divide your positive marker score by 46. It indicates the degree of your positivity in pursuit.
- Calculate the ratio of the negative marker you tick to the total marker you were assessed on. Simply put, divide your negative score by 46. It indicates the degree of your negativity in pursuit.
- Any fraction below 1/3 = 1.
- Any fraction between 1/3 and 2/3 = 2.
- Any fraction above 2/3 = 3.
- The charge can then be applied as applicable.

The interpretation can then be deduced as:

+1 = Just Positive

+2 = Very Positive

+3 = Extremely Positive

-1 = Just Negative

-2 = Very Negative

-3 = Extremely Negative

3. Energy Indices in Team Effort
- Check team member against the markers below.
- Where there is higher number of energy markers signifies the dominant energy charge for the moment, whether it is positive (right) or negative (left).

POSITIVE ENERGY MARKERS IN TEAM EFFORT

1	Brings more elation and happiness to the team.
2	Brings more goodwill to the team.
3	Opens doors of opportunities for the team.
4	Brings platforms of expression for innate abilities within the team.
5	Brings goods out of dry or poisoned environment.
6	Enhances good self-esteem and builds confidence within the team.
7	Rejoices when good things happen to others in the team.
8	Shakes off the dust and cannot be held hostage by challenges of life.
9	Takes responsibility, even when it can be easily shifted to other team members.
10	Seeks solution always, even if it won't be found.
11	Happy times are more than moody times in the team.
12	Makes effort to detach from and let go of a bad past in the team

13	Makes efforts to wipe out bad memories about team members.
14	Not a prisoner of personal mistakes in team tasks.
15	Not an amplifier of mistakes of others in team tasks.
16	Desirable as team mate.
17	Uses gifts, talents, and endowments for general good of the team.
18	Good sense of gratitude.
19	Enjoys life and living happily.
20	Looks strong and feels healthy even in the face of a health challenge.
21	Makes more friends even among difficult team members.
22	Binding agent within theteam.
23	Lights up the party.
24	Good to have around when others are down in the team.
25	Good to have around when team is celebrating.
26	Makes competitive activities within the team fun even when challenging for mastery.
27	Uses personal choices of affirmations such as faith and religion to promote unity.
28	Uses personal choices of affirmations such as faith and religion to benefit others.
29	Uses human differences such as nationalities, tribes, and races to appreciate diversities in the team and humanity.
30	Rationalises and weighs consequences on the team.

31	Measures words and actions in anger to forestall irreparable damage and destruction within the team.
32	Focuses on cause and effect.

33	Good team player in task so required.
34	Team goal supersedes personal ambition.
35	Constructive critic aimed at helping recipient improve.
36	Loves unity and harmony in the group.
37	Happy if others in the team have the most attention.
38	Knows that it owes the team the needed performance and responsibility.
39	Easily shares the glory of the outcome of team efforts.
40	Feels at home in high-performance environment.
41	Exits the team with minimal loss or damage if leaving is inevitable.
42	Leaves great and awesome memories behind.

NEGATIVE ENERGY MARKERS IN TEAM EFFORT

1	Builds up more frustration and depression within the team.
2	Generates repulsion from and towards others in the team.
3	Shuts doors of opportunities for the team.
4	Meets with brick wall at every turn in the team.
5	Poisons good team environments and makes them dry and toxic.
6	Destroys good self-esteem and nose dives confidence within the team.
7	Indifferent to good news and even can be sadistic.
8	Plays the victim and employs emotional blackmail for expression.
9	Plays blame game, even when it is inconsequential.
10	Avoids solution even if it glaringly stares everyone in the face.
11	Moody times dominates the very rare and occasional happy times.
12	Attached to the bad past and bring it up at the slight opportunity.
13	Revels in building infinite storage capacity for recollection of bad done by the team.
14	Cannot look or move past personal mistakes while in the team.

15	Cannot let the mistakes of others pass through any narrow gate.
16	Not-so-desirable team mate.
17	Sees gifts, talents, and endowments as exclusive rights and not privileges.
18	Serious sense of entitlement as a team member.
19	Resents life and always angry about going on in the team.
20	Looks weak and feels moribund even when nothing is wrong within the team.
21	Makes more enemies even among friendly team members.
22	Scattering agent within the team.
23	Sullen and fouls up the team party.
24	Makes team members feel worse in down moments.
25	May dampen the team atmosphere suddenly.
26	Makes competitive activities within the team very toxic.
27	Uses faith and religion as excuse for hatred and team destruction.
28	Uses faith and religion as bottleneck against productivity and progress in team task.
29	Uses nationality, tribes, and races to promote hatred, division, exploitation, and bigotry within the team.
30	Irrational with no regard for consequences.
31	Uses words and actions in anger to cause irreparable damage and destruction within the team.
32	Focuses on luck, conspiracies, and mysteries among team members.

33	Solo, selfish, and individualistic in whatever requires team effort.
34	Personal ambition supersedes team goal.
35	Destructive critic aimed at pulling recipient down.
36	Craves quarrel and chaos in the team.
37	Toxic attention seeking at all cost.
38	Has undue sense of importance above everyone else in the team.
39	Sits upon and personalises the glory of team efforts.
40	Feels lost and persecuted in high-performance environment.
41	Tries hard for the team to collapse upon exit.
42	Leaves wounds and tears behind upon exit.

- Check the dominant marker by comparing how many is ticked in either section. A simple majority indicates dominant positive or negative energy in team effort.
- Calculate the ratio of the positive marker you tick to the total positive marker you were assessed on. Simply put, divide the positive marker score by 42. This indicates the degree of positivity in team effort.
- Calculate the ratio of the negative marker you tick to the total marker you were assessed on. Simply put, divide the negative score by 42. This indicates the degree of negativity in team effort.
- Any fraction below 1/3 = 1.
- Any fraction between 1/3 and 2/3 = 2.
- Any fraction above 2/3 = 3.
- The charge can then be applied as applicable.

The interpretation can then be deduced as:

+1 = Just Positive
+2 = Very Positive
+3 = Extremely Positive
-1 = Just Negative
-2 = Very Negative
-3 = Extremely Negative

4. Energy Indices in Leadership
- Check against the markers below.
- Where there is higher number of energy markers signifies the dominant energy charge for the moment, whether it is positive (right) or negative (left).

POSITIVE ENERGY MARKERS IN LEADERSHIP

1	Brings more elation and happiness to the subordinates.
2	Brings goodwill to the followers.
3	Opens doors of opportunities for the subordinates.
4	Brings platforms of expression for innate abilities of the followers.
5	Brings goods out of dry or poisoned environment.
6	Enhances good self-esteem and builds confidence of the subordinates.
7	Rejoices when good things happen to the followers.
8	Helps subordinates shake off the dust so that they are not held hostage by challenges of life.
9	Takes responsibility, even when it can be easily shifted downward or sideways.
10	Helps and encourages followers to always seek solution to challenges, even if it won't be found
11	Happy times are more than moody times amongst followers and subordinates.
12	Makes effort to detach from and let go of a bad past of the subordinates..
13	Makes efforts to wipe out bad memories about the subordinates.

14	Not a prisoner of own or followers personal mistakes.
15	Not an amplifier of mistakes of the subordinates.
16	Desirable employer and productive leader.
17	Uses gifts, talents, and endowments for general good of the followers.
18	Good sense of gratitude towards subordinates no matter how low in the hierarchy.
19	Enjoys life, living happily and wants same for the followers.
20	Looks strong and feels healthy even in the face of a health challenge to boost followers confidence and morale.
21	Makes more friends even among subordinates.
22	Binding agent among followers.
23	Lights up the party with aura void of arrogance.
24	Good to have around when followers are down.
25	Good to have around when celebrating subordinate's success and achievements.
26	Makes competitive activities fun even when challenging for mastery as the leader.
27	Uses personal choices of affirmations such as faith and religion for character evolvement to be better leader.
28	Uses personal choices of affirmations such as faith and religion to benefit followers and make them get better.
29	Uses human differences such as nationalities, tribes, and races to appreciate diversities in humanity and treat followers fairly and equally..

30	Rational and weighs consequence of actions on the followers.
31	Measures words and actions in anger to forestall irreparable damage to the subordinates or destruction of institution.
32	Focuses on cause and effects when dealing with followers and subordinates.
33	Ssupportive leader, and great boss.
34	Uses power to alleviate and promote.
35	Seeks and pursues peace at all cost.
36	Allows for development and evolvement of subordinates.
37	Boosts confidence of the subordinates.
38	Helps subordinates build positive image.
39	Protects subordinates in time of crisis.
40	Uses open affirmation more often towards subordinates.
41	Good rewarder with appropriate financial rewards such as wages, bonuses and increments.
42	Loyal and good rewarder of loyalty.

NEGATIVE ENERGY MARKERS IN LEADERSHIP

1	Builds up more frustration and depression among subordinates.
2	Generates repulsion.

3	Shuts doors of opportunities against followers or subordinates.
4	Erects brick wall at every turn to frustrate others.
5	Poisons good environments and makes them dry and toxic for subordinates to thrive and flourish.
6	Destroys good self-esteem and nose dives the confidence of subordinates to enjoy control.
7	Indifferent to good news about subordinates and even can be sadistic.
8	Plays the victim and employs emotional blackmail for expression, even when in control.
9	Plays blame game, even when it is inconsequential.
10	Avoids solution for ego sake even if it glaringly stares everyone in the face.
11	Moody times in the presence of the followers/subordinates. dominates the very rare and occasional happy times.
12	Obsessed with the bad past of the subordinates up at the slight opportunity.
13	Revels in building infinite storage capacity for recollection of bad done by subordinates
14	Cannot look or move past subordinates personal mistakes without escalating it.
15	Uses maximum measure of retribution and punishment, even when it is not compulsory.
16	Not-so-desirable employer with poor leadership style.
17	Sees positions and appointments as exclusive rights and not privileges.

18	Serious sense of bossiness.
19	Resents subordinates and always angry about something.
20	Loves weak and moribund subordinates. Feels threatened by agile and lively ones.
21	Makes more enemies out of subordinates·
22	Scattering agent amongst followers and subordinates.
23	Fouls up the party with air of arrogance.
24	Makes subordinates feel worse in their down moments.
25	May dampen the atmosphere suddenly to feel in charge.
26	Makes competitive activities very toxic to stay in control.
27	Uses faith and religion as excuse for opposing and destroying subordinates.
28	Uses faith and religion as excuse to breed hatred in followers and subjects.
29	Uses nationality, tribes, and races to promote division, hatred, exploitation, and bigotry with injustice and lack of equity and fairness.
30	Irrational with no regard for consequences of action on followers.
31	Uses words and actions in anger to cause irreparable damage of subordinates and destruction of institutions.
32	Paranoid and always suspicious of the subordinates.
33	Cantankerous leader, and horrible boss.

34	Uses power as instrument of suppression and oppression.
35	Starts wars or keeps drumming for war without considering human and organisational cost.
36	Cannot stand another rising star.
37	Takes away and destroys the confidence of the subordinates.
38	Revels at the humiliation of subordinates.
39	Saves own head alone at the expense of the team.
40	Uses open condemnations more often towards subordinates.
41	Poor rewarder with appropriate financial rewards such as wages, bonuses and increments.
42	Disloyal and poor rewarder of loyalty.

- Calculate the ratio of the positive marker you tick to the total positive marker you were assessed on. Simply put, divide your positive marker score by 42. This indicates the degree of positivity in leadership.
- If the energy charge is negative, calculate the ratio of the negative marker you tick to the total marker you were assessed on. Simply put, divide your negative score by 42. This indicates the degree of negativity in leadership.

- Any fraction below 1/3 = 1.
- Any fraction between 1/3 and 2/3 = 2.
- Any fraction above 2/3 = 3.
- The charge can then be applied as applicable.

The interpretation can then be deduced as:

+1 = Just Positive
+2 = Very Positive
+3 = Extremely Positive
-1 = Just Negative
-2 = Very Negative
-3 = Extremely Negative

5. Energy Indices in Relationship

- Check against the marker below.
- Where there is higher number of energy markers signifies the dominant energy charge for the moment, whether it is positive (right) or negative (left).

POSITIVE ENERGY MARKERS IN RELATIONSHIP

1	Brings more elation and happiness to the relationship.
2	Brings goodwill to the partner.
3	Opens doors of opportunities for the partner.
4	Brings platforms of expression for innate abilities of the partner.
5	Brings goods out of dry or poisoned relationship.
6	Enhances good self-esteem and builds confidence in the partner.
7	Rejoices when good things happen to the others party.
8	Help the other party to shake off the dust and not to be held hostage by challenges of life.
9	Takes responsibility, even when it can be easily shifted to the partner.
10	Seeks solution to relationship challenges always, even if it won't be found.
11	Happy times are more than moody times in the relationship.
12	Makes effort to detach from and let go of a bad past in the relationship.
13	Makes efforts to wipe out bad memories of past relationships.
14	Don't hold others as prisoners of own mistake.
15	Not an amplifier of mistakes of the partner.
16	Desirable partner.

17	Uses endowments for the utmost benefit of the relationship.
18	Good sense of gratitude for goodwill received.
19	Enjoys life, living happily and wants same for others in the relationship.
20	Looks strong and feels healthy even in the face of a health challenge.
21	Makes relationship more of friendship than a mere contract.
22	Binding agent.
23	Lights up the party of friendship/relationship.
24	Good to have around when partner is down.
25	Good to have around when partner is celebrating.
26	Makes competitive activities fun even when challenging for mastery.
27	Uses personal choices of affirmations such as faith and religion for relationship evolvement.
28	Uses personal choices of affirmations such as faith and religion to benefit partner.
29	Uses human differences such as nationalities, tribes, and races to appreciate diversities in humanity.
30	Rational and weighs consequences of actions on other the party in the friendship/relationship.
31	Measures words and actions in anger to forestall irreparable damage and destruction.
32	Focuses on cause and effects.
33	Makes great and good things happen for others.
34	Leaves people in a better position than when they met.

35	Enhances friendship and love.
36	Loves to make people look and feel that they are better than they actually are.
37	Cares about the feelings of others
38	Looks after the interest of others.
39	Empathetic and compassionate.
40	Stands up for those who are less privileged.
41	Enters relationship to give and receive love.
42	Has regard for associations.
43	Has respect for human web and connectivity.
44	Full of goodwill and appreciation towards humanity and fellow human.
45	Argues and maintains cordiality to keep relationships.

NEGATIVE ENERGY MARKERS IN RELATIONSHIP

1	Builds up more frustration and depression in relationship.
2	Generates repulsion from and towards partner.
3	Shuts doors of opportunities against partner.
4	Creates brick wall within the relationship, making closeness impossible.
5	Poisons good environments and makes them dry and toxic for healthy relationship.
6	Destroys good self-esteem and nose dives the confidence of partner.
7	Indifferent to good news about relationship and even can be sadistic towards partner.

8	Plays the victim and employs emotional blackmail for expression against partner. .
9	Plays blame game, even when it is inconsequential to the relationship reality on ground.
10	Avoids solution to conflicts in relationship even if it glaringly stares everyone in the face.
11	Moody times dominates the very rare and occasional happy times in relationship.
12	Attached to the bad past relationship(s) and brings it up at the slightest opportunity.
13	Revels in building infinite storage capacity for recollection of bad done to them by partner.
14	Cannot look or move past personal mistakes.
15	Cannot let the mistakes of partner pass through any narrow gate.
16	Not-so-desirable as partner.
17	Uses endowments as instruments of control, manipulation and oppression in friendship/relationship.
18	Serious sense of entitlement in relationship.
19	Resents life and always angry about something.
20	Looks weak and feels moribund even when nothing is wrong in order to gain attention or exercise control.
21	Makes more enmity than friendship with partner in the relationship.
22	Scattering agent.
23	Sullen and fouls up the party for the partner.
24	Makes partner feel worse in down moments.
25	May dampen the atmosphere suddenly in order to gain partner's attention.

26	Makes competitive activities very toxic with friends/partner.
27	Uses faith and religion as excuse for relationship destruction.
28	Uses faith and religion as excuse to breed hatred and not love in partner.
29	Uses nationality, tribes, and races to promote hatred, exploitation, and bigotry towards friends/partner.
30	Irrational with no regard for consequences.
31	Uses words and actions in angers to cause irreparable damage and destruction.
32	Paranoid and too suspicious.
33	Fouls up others' aura with unnecessary arguments or pettiness.
34	Messes up people's day and life ultimately.
35	Breeds bitterness, resentment, and hatred among other parties associated with the friendship or partnership.
36	Loves to put others down in order to appear better.
37	Cares less about whose ox is gored when seeking gratifications.
38	Too engrossed in self and cannot look after anyone else.
39	Callous and merciless especially in vital decision making.
40	Takes advantage of whoever is less privileged in the relationship.
41	Enters relationships to use or torment someone.
42	Isolated and menace to associations of any kind.
43	Disconnected from and dangerous to human community.

44	Full of bile, hatred and resentment towards humanity and fellow human.
45	Argues with expletives in order to ruin relationships.

- Calculate the ratio of the positive marker you tick to the total positive marker you were assessed on. Simply put, divide the positive marker score by 45. This indicates the degree of positivity being brought into the relationship.
- Calculate the ratio of the negative marker you tick to the total marker you were assessed on. Simply put, divide the negative score by 45. This indicates the degree of negativity being brought into the relationship.

- Any fraction below 1/3 = 1.
- Any fraction between 1/3 and 2/3 = 2.
- Any fraction above 2/3 = 3.
- The charge can then be applied as applicable.

The interpretation can then be deduced as:
 +1 = Just Positive
 +2 = Very Positive
 +3 = Extremely Positive
 -1 = Just Negative
 -2 = Very Negative
 -3 = Extremely Negative

The Place of Energy Indices in Self-Assessment

At every given time and on any given assignment, you must be able to assess whether your energy disposition is negative and whether the energy level you are dealing with is sufficient for the desired result.

- *Negative energy will produce negative results and influence even when it is available in low quantum.*
- *Positive energy will produce positive result and influence.*
- *Low positive energy level will produce low drive and achieve just little.*
- *Low positive energy may be insufficient for the necessary drive at times.*
- *High positive energy will maximise the chance to extract results and exact influence.*
- *High negative energy will simply sap life out of anything it dominates.*

The Place of Energy Indices in Team Appraisal

Team members, and in particular team leaders, must be able to appraise the energy charge and the energy level of the team in delivering its mandate. Individual energy involvement must also be appraised. We must not shy away from this candid appraisal. A team withers away towards death when the right energy is missing in the right quantity. This will help determine:

- *The cumulative charge and what level of energy the team is operating on.*
- *Who is contributing what in energy charge and in what quantum?*
- *What is everyone's level of involvement in mandate delivery.*

- *Places of need for team energy improvement.*
- *Places of need for individual energy improvement.*
- *Progress or depreciation in team energy charge and level.*
- *Who is changing for better and who is not improving or getting worse?*
- *Who is to be kept in the team as much as possible?*
- *Who is to be dropped from the team like hot potato?*
- *What kind of energy charge and level to add as desirable and look out for when recruiting new team member?*
- *Rewards and promotions.*
- *Right leadership appointments.*

The Place of Energy Indices When Relating

Truthful appraisal of the charge and level of energy you and the one(s) you are relating with bring into the relationship is necessary here. This applies from friendships to marital relationships. The charge and quantum check go a long way in determining:

- *Energy differentials and compatibility in relating.*
- *Resolving differentials.*
- *Building on compatibility.*
- *Readiness to make the relationship work or let go.*
- *Continuous improvement on standing relationship.*

Wherever you find yourself, either by nature or design, there is always room for the right energy migration. You can always work your way across the divide from negative to positive and from barely positive to extremely positive. You can always move in the right energy direction. Energy charge is real and being positive is always better.

Lesson #32–Always strive to make the right energy migration.

Kind regards.